ACCOLADES FOR ... ...

In his book *At-One-Ment: Reclaiming Our Humanity*, Peter J Hughes summons us with a wake-up call to reclaim the heart and soul of our humanity. Through straight talk, insightful story-telling, and practical action points, Peter's delightful and often wicked sense of humor, direct yet loving guidance, and old soul wisdom help make waking up to our higher potential a nurturing as well as powerful transition. You must read this now!

—Sonia Choquette, New York Times Best Selling Author of *The Answer Is Simple ... Love Yourself, Live Your Spirit* and *Ask Your Guides*

At-One-Ment is an exceptional book that will lighten your heart and feed your soul. Through humor, relatable stories, and deep wisdom, Peter teaches how to understand life both within and outside of yourself. The flow, the guidance, and the energy behind the words will change your soul.

—Dianne Maroney, RN, MSN, The Imagine Project, Inc.

For those prepared to generate more love, abundance, and joy in their lives, *At-One-Ment: Reclaiming Our Humanity* is a great guide. Peter's straight talk, lighthearted stories, and action points inspire us to remember the light within ourselves as well as how to share our unique gifts with the world.

—Sydney Price, Founder and CEO, The Knew Purpose

A longtime seeker of personal transformation, I am excited and inspired by this beautiful, sensitive guidebook. From cave drawings to allegories and fables, stories capture and catapult the human experience. Peter Hughes illustrates through story how simple actions, grounding us in the present, will transform us and our perceptions—if we allow—and by consequence, transform our greater world. With much anticipation, I look forward to my own evolving At-One-Ment, putting each Action Point into daily practice. By savoring each moment on our journey to joy and surrender, we are led to happy, fulfilled thriving!

—Marianne Wunch, Film Producer

With humor, compassion, and deep honesty, Peter J Hughes lays out a practical and inspiring guide for how we might show up with soulful purpose to meet the challenges of our times. As a practicing psychologist, I appreciate Peter's deep insight into what it takes to shift from our old stories to new, or reclaimed, versions of ourselves. In my role as an adult educator, I am awed by his ability to convey concepts so that they connect with people on a cognitive, emotional, and spiritual level, all at once. Peter's light shines bright. As a long-lived seeker, I find his guidance to be transformational.

—Helen Hand, PhD, President of Colorado Free University, Denver's premier adult education center offering in-person and online lifelong learning since 1987

AT-ONE-MENT

RECLAIMING OUR HUMANITY

PETER J HUGHES

At-One-Ment: Reclaiming Our Humanity
Published by Delahues Productions, Inc.
Denver, Colorado

ISBN: 978-1-7372945-0-4
SELF-HELP / Motivational & Inspirational

Cover and Interior design by Victoria Wolf,
wolfdesignandmarketing.com. Copyright owned by Peter J Hughes

Publisher's Cataloging-in-Publication data
Names: Hughes, Peter J, author.
Title: At-one-ment : reclaiming our humanity / Peter J Hughes.
Description: Denver, CO: Delahues Productions, inc, 2021.
Identifiers: ISBN: 978-1-7372945-0-4
Subjects: LCSH Self-actualization (Psychology). | Humanity. | Self-help
techniques. | Conduct of life. | Change (Psychology). | BISAC SELF-
HELP / Motivational & Inspirational
Classification: LCC BJ1589 .H84 2021 | DDC 170/.44--dc23

Companies, professional groups, clubs, and other organizations may
qualify for special terms when ordering quantities of this title. For
information, email: delahues@msn.com;

Printed in the United States of America.

PJH

To my beautiful friend Laura DiMinno who, in her transition, held open the veil between Heaven and Earth so that I might look upon infinity and further re-member the Light of Who I Am. I feel your guidance always and in all ways as we continue our journey through this magnificent adventure, eternally *Spirit in Session*.

CONTENTS

PART FOUR: MASTERING OUR HUMANITY

AT-ONE-MENT: RECLAIMING OUR HUMANITY

"The state of the world does not dictate the experience of our humanity, but rather, the state of humanity informs our experience of the world. The world as a mirror reflects back to us the version of ourselves we project onto it. When we project a Soulful awareness of our humanity onto the world, we create a thriving Soulfilled experience of ourselves. When we project a Soulless experience of our humanity onto the world, we manifest a Soulless experience of ourselves. Our free will guarantees we are never judged in what we choose. However, we are always—and in all ways—honored, supported, and held accountable in what we have chosen."

Vibe Tune Up: Spinning Fear Into Love
(01/17)
Peter J Hughes

PREFACE

AT-ONE-MENT

Time to Wake Up

LIFE IS FULL OF DEFINING MOMENTS, opportunities to consider our options and choose once again how we show up in the world and what realities we create. The morning of November 9, 2016, was one such defining moment for me. On that day, I found myself in the process of waking with a sense of intense devastation, which I was not, in that moment, prepared or willing to confront and process. I was clear this was deeper than the disappointment of "my preferred candidate" not winning an election, as I understand and honor how democracy works— sometimes you win, sometimes not. So, I was able to isolate out that part of my emotions. But this feeling that the whole world had lost its mind and the very Soul of humanity had been jeopardized was beyond anything I could wrap my mind or heart around. This was bigger than the outcome of an election and ran deeper than who was right or who was wrong.

Being empathic, intuitive, and imaginative by nature (all of which are tools I have developed in my career as a life-enhancing facilitator, spiritual teacher, and stage director), I knew if I was feeling this deeply out of sorts, disconnected, and unable to ground myself, something monumental was occurring. I honestly didn't know if I had it in me to face what we had queued up for our cultural, national, and global path.

I have navigated my share of walks through the dark side of the human experience—having hit rock bottom, lying broken and bloody, and knowing which way was up only because I had landed on my back. Nothing is more unnerving and disorienting for an empath/introvert than feeling disconnected from the internal guidance of my faith. And on this morning, I found I had landed face down in overwhelming despair, unlike anything I could reference.

So, I had a conversation with God. Lying in bed curled up in the fetal position, the covers pulled up over my ears and around my head, I announced with a sense of profound defeat, "I can't do this. I don't want to be here in this world anymore." This moment had presented itself on the tail end of four years of intense life experiences that had left me depleted and, at times, struggling to grab on to my faith, feeling raw and fatigued. "So, I'm not moving from this spot until You give me a clear understanding of the part You want me to play in the healing of all this chaos ... and Your reassurance that You are going to be there guiding me each step of the way through this."

Five hours would pass before I stirred in my cocoon, the angle of the sunlight streaming through the divide in the bedroom window curtains indicating it was now midday. I could hear birds calling to each other from the trees in the back yard and our dogs exchanging barks with their neighboring counterparts, a reminder that their lives had not been affected at all by any of this. So far, anyway.

As I awoke, I felt a sense of, if not peace, at least purpose in my mind and heart. I didn't know exactly what had happened, but I knew the reality of the election results had not changed. The sense of chaos triggered by the results still had, as I saw it, a chokehold on the heart of our country and—somehow—on our humanity. This day was indeed the beginning of a journey we individually and collectively were going to take. And as much as people needed to believe it was all "the other side's fault," the truth was we were in this together.

Sitting up in bed, it was clear to me. I, like everyone, had a part to play in all of this—a contribution to honor and a purpose to fulfill. My life's journey to date, and my work as a life-enhancement facilitator and spiritual teacher, had prepared me for this. Even—and especially—my work as a stage director (leading a team through the creative process to manifested desired results) had trained me to step up into this purposeful work. I had an intuitive knowing and, without understanding the details of *how*, knew we were not only going to *survive* this storm but—depending on how we played our cards—we would come out the other side having redefined our potential to *thrive*. I was assured of this understanding in my head, and I trusted the guidance in my heart.

A teaching in *A Course in Miracles* says that everything is either Love or a call for Love, and the appropriate response to both is Love. This insight invites us to consider that when someone is "acting out," they are doing so in reaction to their experience of a perceived disconnect from Love. "Acting out" is a desperate call for Love created by a hunger to feel connected—a hunger so strong that even if the connection is manifest in violence, we would rather be abused than ignored. When we act and react in Love, we dispel the illusion of separation and honor our eternal connection, and in this, we heal the multitude of perceived gaps we have created between us.

Our cultural experience over the time leading up to the morning of November 9, 2016, had been fueled by a gradual dehumanizing of each other in the name of righteousness. This fear-based pattern was nothing new to the human experience, as history has repeatedly shown this behavior to be consciously and intentionally practiced as part of the art of manipulating a culture mindset to obtain and retain control of the masses. However, this time I sensed we had reached a peak—a tipping point unlike any other time in the history of our humanity. With the progress in technology and the ability to communicate globally in a matter of seconds, we were forced to wake up individually and collectively in "real time." The Soul of our humanity had reached its limit for accommodating fear-driven fatigue and was held hostage by a toxic perception of lack and the delusion of separation. It was no longer appropriate for us to remain in a deep sleep of complacency and continue to hit the snooze button on the awakening of our potential. We were queued up for a breakthrough in our evolution—the likes of which would forever change the world as we knew it. It would either reveal a thriving version of ourselves that we were designed for but had not yet imagined possible—or trigger the slow death of our democracy along with our humanity. Everything was in place to support us in this shift of collective consciousness, and the choice was ours as to which way it would play out.

Sitting on the side of the bed, I was curious as to why we couldn't have chosen a smoother, more graceful, enlightened version of our awakening process. Bowing my head, I surrendered. "Oh well, we didn't. We have chosen this version; there's no point in resisting. Let's get to it." I knew I had my part to do: my part assigned to me by God in God's plan. For now, that part looked like closing the perceived gaps between us by hitting the reset button on our humanity. Only when we change our mind about what's possible are we in a position to change the world. In that moment, I had done my part to change *my* mind, and now it was time for me to sit up, suit up, and show up—to realign with Atonement and get into action with our At-One-Ment—reclaiming our humanity.

INTRODUCTION

STEPPING UP ON PURPOSE

Getting Into Action

I AM ONE WHO IS HAPPIEST when I'm serving in purpose. Whether teaching a class, facilitating a workshop, directing a stage production, or working one-to-one with private clients, it is an honor and a privilege to witness people blossoming into their potential. The highest of the high for me is being present when someone rewrites their story of limitation, breaks through the walls of resistance, and steps into the version of themselves not previously considered a possibility—yet always waiting to be claimed.

I am wired for seeing the Light of people, their goodness, their Soul, their humanity, if you will. The quality has been present in me since my earliest memories. I was not trained in empathy, compassion, insight, and intuition, but rather, they came to me naturally. However, like many of us, experience and familial training conditioned me to survive the game of life. My parents and other influential adults gave me the best of what they had to offer. It was grounded in the stories they crafted about how the real world worked, and it was based on what they were told, what they experienced themselves, and what they claimed to know for sure.

Much of this "survival" training and what I witnessed in people's personality, actions, and words ran counter to what I was seeing and experiencing as someone who recognized the Light in each person. The Light of people's Souls did not match what they believed about themselves. This contradiction was a confusing experience for me as a child and young adult until I began the informal and formal training of my personal awakening process.

I remember being introduced to a colleague of my father's when I was five years old. When the man leaned down toward me and reached out to shake my hand, I became overwhelmed with emotions and started to cry (an experience for which I was labeled sensitive, shy, and weak). I didn't understand it at the time, but I later came to see that the emotions that had overwhelmed me were not mine; they belonged to this man. It would be years later before I would hear how he had embezzled money from the business in which he and my father were partners, a business that eventually went bankrupt.

It might make sense how, as a sensitive child, I could have picked up on this gentleman's vibe, and in my five-year-old mind, I could tell he was a bad man. But that's not the story with which my five-year-old mind connected. I felt he was a good man who was doing bad things because he didn't believe in himself. I did not have the words for it at the time; however, I felt how he couldn't grasp his Light and was lost in the dark of his story, his training, and his beliefs about how the real world worked. I cried, not so much because I could feel his pain, but more so because I had become overwhelmingly disoriented by the vastness of the gap between what he believed to be the truth about himself and the truth of his Light and his Soul potential.

Over the years, I would struggle with my own survival training and stories of limitation—at times not able to grasp my Light through the filters of inherited beliefs that didn't fit. I wasn't wired for the struggle of surviving, and I had not been nurtured in the grace of thriving. Judgment of myself overflowed into projecting judgment onto others, a practice that backfired on me more times than not, as karma tends to do.

Finding a balance in navigating the Light in each of us, and the stories we tell ourselves, would eventually come to me after I had done the work to claim the clarity necessary to sustain the balance. My desire to achieve a balance was the first step, and, having committed to the journey, I found my natural state of empathy, compassion, insight, and intuition brought me to rendezvous with teachers and teachings that helped me master this balancing act. Like all master training, I first had to do the work of cleaning up the messes I had made along the way, rewriting my story about the facts of my life experiences, and rewiring my beliefs about my Light and my Soul potential.

I find comfort in knowing we are all works in progress and am humbled in accepting that, as far as I have come in my awakening process, there is always more life to explore and more clarity to unveil. This discovery is one reason why I love doing my purpose work of teaching and facilitating; we teach what we know, and by teaching it, we know more.

Sitting on the side of the bed that morning in November 2016, I knew I had my part to do, my part assigned to me by God in God's plan. For now, that part looked like pressing the reset button on our humanity. I was practiced in changing my mind about what's possible for myself, and I had years of experience in facilitating people in changing their minds about what was possible for themselves. Now, it seemed I was being called into service in a way I had not yet considered. I was being guided to reach beyond the intimate classroom, the borders of my cozy office, and the creative cocoon of the rehearsal space. I would be stepping up on purpose, as I had never stepped up before, in search of the Light of our humanity, the Soul of our potential. And even though I didn't know where this journey would take me, I had my Light to lead the way, and I trusted it.

Throughout human history, each dark age has been followed by a renaissance, a time of reinventing ourselves and the expression of our humanity. Our current situation and the unknown of what is yet to come are no exception. The sense of pending chaos and struggle I felt that morning was so intense; I knew this was something we had to go through, and there was no way around it. My thriving training had taught me that at such times as this, it served me well to reference one of my favorite default questions in any situation: "What is this all trying to show me, the seeing of which will change everything?" This question always pivots me in the direction of the answers that move me forward, lifting me out of feeling overwhelmed and stuck and raising me into the possibility that comes with change.

I was curious how I could position myself to thrive through this dark age, which would, by Divine design, lead us to the next renaissance and new expression of our humanity. I considered the questions: "Who do I want to be on the other side of this, and who can I start being *now* to prepare myself to be ready and able to claim and sustain it when I get there?" From here, I was inspired to look at how we, as a collective humanity, can begin the process of unlearning what we have accepted as the truth of how the real world works. If what we have been *taught to think* influenced the boundaries of what we had *come to accept as possible*, and if what we had *come to believe was possible* informed what *we accepted as the truth*, then what would it take for us to begin *introducing new thoughts*, which would evolve into *new beliefs*, which would emerge as *our new truth*? *(Please read that through several times until it flows, and you feel it "click" for you.)*

There was a time not that long ago when people accepted as truth the belief that the Earth was flat. And why not? There was no reference to support thinking or believing otherwise ... until there was. Today, though some still believe it to be flat, this idea seems absurd to most. Yet when a flat world is all you know, you don't know to know something else. Had the Earth changed its shape when the new facts were introduced? Of course not. Did the old belief about the shape of our planet shift when the new thought, informed from a broader perspective, was introduced? Yes. It took a while, and a number of people were imprisoned and/or executed for challenging the old belief in the process, but over time, people would begin to teach the new thought, accept the new belief, and settle into the new truth.

If we have landed where we are today because of our chronic unconscious individual and collective thinking, then what would it take to consciously change our thoughts about who we think we are, redefine our potential, and be willing to tap into a version of ourselves not yet considered? With my curiosity ignited, these questions filled my waking hours and paraded through my dreams at night.

What if a belief in separateness, similar to a belief in a flat world, had become our truth because it was what we were taught, what we learned, and the only thing we knew? And, what if our humanity, like the round Earth, had an unalterable truth and unbreakable connectedness? What if it were possible only for us to *believe* we are separate but impossible for us to be anything but connected? And what if, to course-correct our path, all we need to do is relearn our way back into alignment with the truth of our humanity, our At-One-Ment?

Ideas were planted and took root, inspiring me to write a series of articles for my monthly *Your Vibe Alignment Tune Up* newsletter. The articles were introduced as a campaign for *A Year of Reclaiming Our Humanity*, inviting readers to enjoy an assortment of stories encouraging us to consider how we might change our perspective on the potential of our humanity. Along with a short story, each article included practical action points: practices to implement during the month between articles, with the intention that if we took the time to practice these thoughts for the thirty days, we could change how we relate to our humanity individually and collectively.

The monthly installment of articles, each with three action points, supported the idea that it takes twenty-one days to break an old habit while introducing a sustainable replacement habit. Some studies have suggested it could take as many as fifty-nine to ninety-one days to revise a default habit, depending on the habit. The key in any habit-changing process is identifying the trigger, action, and payoff associated with the old habit and replacing it with a new, healthier trigger, action, and payoff. In any case, the month between articles allotted enough time to, if not completely change habits, at least create a platform on which to launch a healthy start.

With each month's article, I became more interested and invested in where the stories and action points were taking us. Each article stood on its own, yet I began to see how the action points were building on each other, unfolding to reveal a bigger plan, a more expansive instruction, a more Divine guidance. It wasn't until the sixth installment, the half-year mark in the year-long campaign, that it was revealed to me how I had been unwittingly writing a book. By this point, it was futile for me to deny or resist the direction of my efforts, as the book was half-written. So, I had to change my mind about what I was doing, rewrite my story about being a (*gulp*) writer, and rewire my thoughts that I was now penning what would eventually become the foundation for *At-One-Ment: Reclaiming Our Humanity*.

Once the *Year of Reclaiming Our Humanity* campaign articles were complete, I was able to see how the first six articles, addressing our primal urge for survival, looked at correcting our individual and collective course toward what I feared would be a total meltdown of our humanity. The second set of six articles, addressing our spiritual urge to thrive, invited us to consider navigating our thoughts, words, and actions into alignment with our natural ability to flourish. So, too, for the book, the first six chapters are an invitation to course-correct our humanity, and the following six chapters are a guideline for claiming and sustaining the expression of our humanity at its highest potential.

Deepak Chopra's lecture series *The Higher Self,* references the idea that it takes three generations to change a belief. I was intrigued by this concept and explored it further. I came to consider how the first generation of the belief-shifting process identifies a disconnect with the old belief yet continues to support (enforce) it. The second generation, having grown restless, rejects the old belief and rises up in resistance, triggering a period of chaos during which new possibilities are considered. The third generation, having been liberated from the old belief as truth and having navigated a process of elimination, starts to settle into ideas that are a more appropriate fit for the evolution of the individual and the collective. In my classes, I use the example of wandering through the desert for forty years in search of the Promised Land. In this metaphor, we consider how the Promised Land is not so much a literal place but rather a mindset, a belief. The forty-year journey is the journey of the three generations it takes to change a belief. The Promised Land is always available; however, it is not accessible until we can see it, and we are unable to see it until we have chosen to believe it. When enough of the third generation (about 52 percent of the tribe) aligns with the new thinking, we arrive at a tipping point that speeds up the momentum of the belief-shift process. When the collective is on board with the new thinking, they embrace the new belief and reveal the Promised Land. This shift shows the power of positive group thought, the influence of our connectedness, the potential of our At-One-Ment, and the reclaiming of our humanity.

The idea of group thought, connectedness, and At-One-Ment of our humanity reminded me of another analogy I had heard over the years from a number of sources. In this analogy, we are invited to consider how we must work together to sustain alignment with the health and wellness of our humanity, much like the cells of our body work together to sustain alignment with physical health and wellness. When the cells are at war with each other, imbalance and chaos set in and lead to disease, which, if not healed, leads to death. Similarly, humans can work together to align with a sustainable health and wellness of our humanity body. When humans work against each other, imbalance and chaos set in and lead to disease, which, if not healed, leads to self-destruction.

As the series of *Reclaiming Our Humanity* articles began to reveal themselves as installations in an At-One-Ment aligning process, the intention and goal of the process became clear to me. Starting with ourselves and projecting through the collective, we could self-select out of our diseased belief of separation and self-select into the beliefs that support our natural state of Oneness. Through choosing our atonement, our all-inclusive connection with Divine Source, we would achieve our At-One-Ment, our all-inclusive connection with each other. And from our place of At-One-Ment, we would claim our humanity at its highest potential fully-realized.

HOW THE BOOK WORKS

The *At-One-Ment: Reclaiming Our Humanity* conversation and experience is designed to support us in the personal process of aligning ourselves with the highest potential of our individual humanity and, by proxy, our collective potential. When we understand that we cannot give what we do not have, we see how important and valuable it is to invest the effort in our self-alignment first, claim our internal healed humanity, and then be the change we wish to see in the world. Then and only then will we achieve a sustainable alignment with our highest potential fully-realized.

The main portion of the book is divided into Four Parts, with each Part containing three chapters. Each chapter is broken down into three sections: Straight Talk, which sets up the main idea and intention of the chapter; Talk Story, which expands on the idea through short-story form; and three suggested Action Points to put the idea on its feet and into action.

The Talk Story and Action Points shared in *At-One-Ment: Reclaiming Our Humanity* are designed to support us in a progressive alignment process. Though the chapters are a whole and complete invitation and instruction in and of themselves, they are designed to build on each other in a progression of sustainable results. Because of this, I recommend starting at the beginning with the guidance and instruction of the first chapter and Action Points and working your way through the chapters in order. However, if you are inspired to navigate the process more randomly, please, by all means, feel free to do so. All that is asked of you is to give the processes a chance, invest the effort to implement the Action Points, and gift yourself the opportunity to adjust and acclimate to a shift in perspective while intending to manifest sustainable results.

As part of the research and development prior to publication, a four-part workshop series for the book provided an opportunity to test the effects of the *At-One-Ment: Reclaiming Our Humanity* conversation and experience. In these workshops, participants found, to varying degrees, the content and guidance to be informational, inspirational, and transformational. Considering that each participant would bring to the workshop experience their own set of intellectual, emotional, and spiritual filters, I was interested to see how accessible and effective the process would be. I found that the degree to which people were willing to try something new and work through resistance greatly influenced the degree to which each manifested significant and sustainable results. Across the board, each participant experienced, to varying degrees, a shift in self-awareness and an awakening to a broader perspective of personal and collective potential. For some, it was a slight shift, and for others, a profound shift. In every case, participants got out of the workshop equal to what they were willing and able to invest.

If, going through the book, you find yourself becoming anxious, distracted, and disinterested, do an authentic check-in with yourself and be clear whether you are unconsciously self-sabotaging your efforts and resisting manifesting life-changing results. Faced with the threat of change, the ego and intellect can be clever in their passive-aggressive efforts to gaslight your focus away from being effective. For instance, you might try to convince yourself you are too busy to make time for practicing the Action Points. However, the Action Points are designed to apply as part of your daily schedule; that's how we change the habit. It doesn't take more time to apply the Action Points. It does, however, take more conscious intention on your part. Do not be deceived by their perceived simplicity. The Action Points are potent in their ability to generate effective results in mind-shift training. Be gentle with yourself and stay the course. Remember, your ego wouldn't be resisting if you weren't queuing up for a profound shift.

Though this process is intended to support anyone with a willingness and desire to reclaim our humanity, I understand it will not be everyone's cup of tea. I am totally good with that. If you find this conversation is not a match for you, and you are authentically not interested in this process, then do yourself a great service and don't push it. Don't waste your energy and time chewing and stewing over what didn't work for you, or why.

As I tell my clients, I have no attachment to if this doesn't work for you, or why it doesn't. What I care about and what I'm passionate about is that you find what *does* work for you. Please don't get hung up on or distracted by what you don't want or what doesn't work for you. Instead, always give your focus to and invest your energy in your continued search of what does work—for you.

So, if this is not for you, put the book down, put your hands in the air, and slowly back away. Consider, instead, paying it forward to someone you feel might appreciate it. Move on to something else that could be the "perfect" something that *does* suit you and be glad for the opportunity to know what doesn't work for you.

However, if you do feel a connection to the process (and resistance, in a way, is a form of connection), keep moving forward, implementing the Action Points with the intention to master the process of reclaiming your humanity.

Whether you've been consciously on your journey for a lifetime, you're just starting out, or you are giving it another try; whether this all makes perfect sense or you think it's all a crock-of-crap—great! Start there. If this *is* your first time at bat with the whole idea of changing your mind and changing the world, do not worry; *At-One-Ment: Reclaiming Our Humanity* is presented with gentle guidance. As is the case with any journey, to be effective, it's always best to start at the beginning.

The first steps are the most important as they give us the opportunity to establish our balance, build our strength, and find our rhythm. If this isn't your first time at the self-improvement rodeo, and you fancy yourself well beyond the contents of the first chapters, I invite you to try a more challenging process by starting with the last chapter and working your way in reverse order to the first chapter. Sometimes, in our expanded spiritual awareness, we can lose touch with our humanness and become ungrounded in the daily business of our physical world experience. Taking a reverse-order approach to these chapters and Action Points can be a great reminder of what you already know and an opportunity to remember to hold yourself accountable for modeling what you already know.

With any process, we are best suited to start with the obvious, the things right in front of us, the things that, to most, would seem too simple and insignificant to be effective. Again, do not be deceived by the perceived simplicity of the power tools the Action Points suggested in this process provide. If you experience resistance to implementing the Action Points (and, trust me, you will experience resistance), I invite you to lean into it rather than pulling back from it. Allow yourself to move through the resistance, knowing that, in doing so, you set yourself up to claim the gold-medal prize that the opportunity holds for you on the other side of the experience.

This effort can seem overwhelming at first if we think it is our job to save the world, fix our community, or manage someone else on their path with the hope that, in doing so, we can prove ourselves worthy of reclaiming our humanity. So let's dispel that delusion of grandeur right off the bat. There is nothing noble about suffering for the greater good of humanity, as suffering is a state of mind requiring a belief that things are hopeless. If we're going to make a difference and contribute to the health and wellness of humanity, it will require us to be at the top of our game with a clear head, an open heart, fearless in faith, and armed with the strength of grace. Remember, this isn't about solving world hunger, finding a cure for cancer, or establishing world peace. Not yet. One miracle at a time. For now, let's focus on being the change we wish to see in the world.

As a stage director and stage/production manager, I have been professionally guiding people through the creative process since 1984. I have been facilitating mind-shift, life-changing, and life-enhancing workshops as my vocation since 2004. In that time, I have had the opportunity to work with participants on a full spectrum of issues—as basic as finding a new job, as intricate as manifesting a life-partner, and as intense as bringing clarity to grieving parents. In all of these situations and every one in between and beyond, we had to find a place to connect, regroup, and launch. No one-size-fits-all formula works for everyone in every situation. That's just the reality of being human. We are works in progress, ever-evolving, on an infinite array of paths. All roads lead to Rome, as the saying goes, and I believe all paths lead home to our Source. In this, I have found our common ground.

The *At-One-Ment: Reclaiming Our Humanity* journey represents a lifetime of personal growth, formal training, and on-the-court application. I offer it here as an outline, a series of touchstones, action points, and performance-enhancement tools to be implemented and developed. I encourage you to think of this process as "Couture for your Soul," an invitation to try it on, see how it fits, then be inspired to make appropriate alterations. In my experience, in order for these ideas and Action Points to work, you have to work *with* them. Likewise, for these ideas and Action Points to be sustainable, you'll need to work consciously and habitually *with* them rather than unconsciously and habitually *against* them.

At-One-Ment: Reclaiming Our Humanity is a journey in reclaiming our individual and collective humanity. Our humanity didn't go anywhere, it didn't disappear, and we didn't displace it. We just forgot to remember it is at the core of who we are as human beings navigating a human experience. The state of our humanity is informed by who we think we are and how we nurture who we believe we are. When we are surviving our humanity, we are doing so on an "empty tank," so to speak. When we are having a thriving experience of ourselves, we breathe thriving life-force into our humanity. Both are appropriate expressions of our individual and collective thoughts, words, and actions. Our thriving humanity is our birthright; the degree to which we choose to thrive is our free will.

So, let's get to work. We've got a journey to take, a process to implement, and our humanity to reclaim.

Onward!

PART ONE
BACK TO BASICS

CHAPTER ONE

IT'S ALWAYS BEST TO START AT THE BEGINNING

-STRAIGHT TALK-

WHEN WE ABANDON THE PRACTICE OF making a conscious effort to appreciate the basics of our daily life or no longer follow the subtle signs that guide us through the world, it is absurd of us to feign confusion and disappointment. Having disconnected from our appreciation of the fundamental touchstones of daily life, we fail to recognize and claim the abundance of opportunities each moment in life has to offer. In this, we severely weaken the foundation of our humanity, and the experience of our individual and collective potential to thrive feels unattainable.

We are energetically connected to everyone and everything at all times and in all ways; this is the One-ness the master teachers have spoken of for thousands of years. Appreciation resets our individual awareness of this eternal and all-inclusive connection, working with it rather than against it, and launches us on the first steps along the path of our At-One-Ment and reclaiming our humanity.

Our ability to consciously and intentionally get back to the basics of nurturing our humanity depends on our willingness to get real about how we are participating in our life—to get real about what we're working with and the behaviors we accept, accommodate, and enable, starting with ourselves. Until we take 100 percent responsibility for how we show up in our daily life and take action to course-correct ourselves into alignment with our highest potential, we will not be able to contribute effectively in reclaiming our humanity—individual or collective.

−TALK STORY−

Like so many of us, I have loved the movie *The Wizard of Oz* since I was a child. It has been a source of entertainment and inspiration; it's an example of the courage, heart, brains, and commitment required to face our deepest fears, remember our inner strength, and claim a life beyond what we believed possible. A journey on which, as Glinda the Good Witch instructed (pointing her magic wand toward the first steps along the Yellow Brick Road), it is always best to start at the beginning.

Long before the days of on-demand entertainment or even clunky VHS machines, we children would anxiously await the annual television broadcast of this classic film. Bathed and in our pajamas, we were ready to settle in for Dorothy's magical adventure, our voices warmed up and ready to sing along with the iconic score, and our pillows on standby to cover our faces during the scary parts. It was truly an event. And if you were lucky, you were one of the households with a color TV, making Dorothy's arrival in Munchkinland a glorious Technicolor transformation.

I admit I was a total geek when it came to buying into the full-spectrum experience of Dorothy's adventures in Oz: getting goose bumps with each song, every cell in my body chilled to the core in terror at the arrival of the Wicked Witch of the West. I never failed to generate tears of joy (mixed with an undertow of disappointment) at the end, when, having returned to her Kansas farm, Dorothy exclaims, "Oh, Auntie Em, there's no place like home," cueing the swelling of the music and the rolling of the final credits.

Always one to believe in the magic of possibility, for years, I was in total denial that Dorothy's journey through Oz was a concussion-induced dream. Each year, I would watch as Dorothy took her magical adventure, hoping deep down she might take a different fork in the road and make a different choice when it came time to click her ruby slippers three times and head on home. Any disappointment on my part with Dorothy's return to Kansas was in protest to her having surrendered her Technicolor dream world in order to return to the reality of her black-and-white world of the Midwest. In my child's logic, I equated this "reality" to be a cop-out, void of imagination, lifeless, and without passion. Much like, as it would be made clear to me later on, how I related to the prospect of adulthood and growing up: a surrender to the loss of innocence and the dismissal of the magic of life. "Please, just drop a house on me now."

In my child's mind and heart, I wanted Dorothy to stay with her friends in the magnificent and colorful merry old land of Oz. Year after year, when the movie ended and I was tucked into bed for the night, I would spend what seemed like hours recommitting to the promise I had made with myself that if being an adult meant I had to surrender my over-the-rainbow childlike wonder, I wanted nothing to do with it. Adulting, as I witnessed it in the grown-ups around me, was a lot of hard work and not a lot of fun. Dorothy was stuck in her celluloid loop and destined to make the same choice for eternity. If she couldn't rewrite her story, perhaps I could rewrite it for both of us by holding on to my childhood.

My metaphoric ruby heels dug in deep. I vowed to make it through the terrible teens with my inner child intact and unscathed. However, a parade of life happenings would derail my covenant, and I began to lose my way in the onslaught of complications, which are the normal and often traumatizing antithesis that comprise the course of adolescence. During my teen years, *The Wizard of Oz* was one of the fantasy worlds I visited to escape and block out the things that were too tough to bear, numbing myself in order to navigate my life without losing my mind. The other kids my age (and younger) were smoking, drinking, acting out sexual curiosity, and experimenting with drugs. Oz was my crack. It wasn't until I was in my later teens, when my inner Dorothy, looking more and more like Bette Davis in *Whatever Happened to Baby Jane*, that I sucked it up, got "real," and abandoned any hope of my more desired alternate ending to Dorothy's adventure.

Resigned to life as it was actually playing out ("But you are in a wheelchair, Blanche!"), I surrendered myself to the realization that I had been pining for a "fantasy" life, which I could not even reach, let alone latch onto with a sustainable grasp. I was living in a constant state of disappointment and anxiety, not being able to manifest the Technicolor life I had imagined for myself all those years ago. As much as I wanted to believe it, I struggled with the idea that "If I ever go looking for my heart's desire again, I won't look any further than my own backyard. Because if it isn't there, I never really lost it to begin with." Instead, I found myself haunted by the Wicked Witch of the West's command to "Surrender, Dorothy" and the possibility that, in my case, if it isn't already there, I never really had it to begin with ... and never would. It would take several more years, a series of intense heartbreaking experiences, and a lot of self-exploration before I stopped relating to Dorothy's backyard in Kansas (and my personal field of dreams) as parched plots of dried-up potential.

In my mid-twenties, I began reframing my Oz issues and what would become the rewiring of my subconscious programming. One day, while between theatre job contracts, I found myself sitting in the dustbowl of my disappointments, buried in a stack of half-read self-help books. Feeling defeated, hopeless, and really sorry for myself, I settled into the couch, picked up the remote control, turned on the television, and slid down the rabbit hole of mind-numbing channel surfing for some mindless distraction. Twenty or so clicks in, I came upon my old favorite movie during the scene where Dorothy meets the Scarecrow. (Have you ever noticed how, during the *If I Only Had a Brain* song, Dorothy's pigtails change length several times? I would one day use that as a sight gag for the Judy Garland character in a murder comedy spoof I directed. Funny thing about inspiration: it happens when and where it happens. But, back to the couch.) So, I settled in to watch *The Wizard of Oz* for the umpteenth time. My spirit lay broken and bloodied, having hit the rock bottom of limbo somewhere between my deflated childhood and a flatlining adulthood. I made it to the final scene in Oz when Glinda informs Dorothy she has always had the power to go home—all she had to do was click her heels three times, and she would be back in Kansas in an instant—and I (((snapped))). For some reason, distinct from any earlier viewing of the film, I had a visceral reaction to Glinda's reveal. My resigned, bitter, and jaded self screamed out, "What?! Are you kidding me?!" Dorothy should have backhanded that glitter bitch and shoved that wand up her ... (((breathe))). I couldn't understand why Dorothy didn't launch into a monological rage of, "What the hell do you mean telling me this (((now)))?! You maybe could have made mention of this back in Munchkinland before I *walked* all this way in these ruby, blister-inducing slippers, stalked by that emerald-skinned douche bag, terrorized by freaky-assed flying fleabags, and all but soiling myself before that shit show of a 'Wonderful' Wizard of Oz moron? WTF is wrong with you, lady?!" (Imagine my surprise when, a few years later, Mad TV did a *Wizard of Oz* alternate ending sketch, which almost word-for-word mirrored my rant.)

In that moment, I shocked myself. "Wow, what was that about?" How had I arrived at this place of crapping on the altar of one of my childhood sacred icons? I turned off the television, reached over, and removed a random selection from the stack of my recently acquired inspirational and self-help books, hopeful I would find some clarity in what this was and how I could navigate some sort of comforting insight. I did find what I was looking for in the form of a confronting bitch-slap of get-real. I had yet to hold myself accountable for how I was showing up in my life and had to get real about my part in what I was working with. I had a rude awakening when I realized my rage-filled outburst stemmed from an unconscious chronic resignation cloaked in cynicism. Having fallen prey to a series of disappointing life-happenings, I was using them to stifle my potential and hide my worth. Similar to Dorothy using Miss Gulch as the reason for her unhappiness, I was using external influences as the source of mine. I had disconnected from my natural wiring to thrive and was using my disappointments to justify not stepping up effectively in my own life. In doing so, I had become deaf to any guidance pointing me in the direction homeward to my authentic self. Though my life was rich with possibility, I couldn't see it; I couldn't hear it. And if someone had told me, like Dorothy, I wouldn't have believed them.

I then thought of Dorothy unleashing her rage on the Wizard when he reneges on his promise to provide support in solving all of their problems, thus preventing the four friends from access to their heart's desires—or so they thought. Recalling the themes addressed in my library of self-help books, I began to connect some dots on how getting to the point of rage can be a profound place of release, relaunch, and healing. Anger has fire to it, where resignation has little, if any, charge. It was *because* of Dorothy's unwillingness to accept disappointment and defeat that she could launch herself beyond what she had previously perceived as limitations. I could, if I chose, deny my own private Kansas, trapped in my rock-bottom-of-the-well perspective, and launch myself upward. The key to the success of my efforts, similar to Dorothy's experience, was to rethink how I related to myself, my life, and myself in my life. To change my mind about who I thought I was and what I was capable of, to align myself with the version of me willing and able to kick serious butt along the yellow brick road of my life. To spin my life events into gold. From this perspective, how I would see and experience the world would shift dramatically, and I could gain access to answers, solutions, and possibilities I would not otherwise have known to consider.

The moment Scarecrow asks Glinda why she didn't tell Dorothy this before, to which Glinda calmly responds, "Because she wouldn't have believed me. She had to find out for herself," made so much more sense to me. It's not that we're too dense or naive to understand; we're just not yet ready to hear the answers and the guidance. We have not yet navigated our way to being in alignment with the clarity that clears the path to our potential. We have work to do to liberate ourselves from our training around thriving and to realign ourselves with the vibration of our potential. Dorothy had to get over it and stop blaming Miss Gulch in order to take down the Wicked Witch of the West, both of whom were manifested metaphorical representations of Dorothy's internal dialogue and beliefs about herself. I, too, had internal work to do—course-correcting and training and rewiring beliefs I had about myself and my potential.

It was in my outburst, sitting in front of the TV that day, that I was able to make my way to the connection and really understand the insight of Glinda's invitation back in Munchkinland, to "start at the beginning." Glinda wasn't floating in a mindless bubble of ethereal goop. She was clear and unapologetically calm in her eternal awareness, immovable with the strength of grace in her belief in the unlimited potential of the human spirit when unharnessed from self-imposed limitation mistaken for truth. Like the masters who have walked the planet throughout human history, Glinda was tapped into a higher consciousness, the perspective from which she guided and facilitated Dorothy on her journey. And it was from here that Glinda's insight was anchored and her guidance offered, which profoundly included the wisdom to hold on to the answers until Dorothy was ready and able to believe their clarity, trust their simplicity, claim them for herself, and act on them.

That same year—1989—*The Wizard of Oz* was rereleased in theaters in celebration of the movie's fiftieth anniversary. I had never seen the film on a big screen and found myself settling into my seat with a rush of childlike anticipation, just as I had all those years ago. As soon as the overture started, I sat straight up, eyes welling with delight and a lump in my throat. And though I sang every song and recited most of the dialogue (apparently along with everyone else in the theater), it was as if I were seeing it for the first time. And in a way, I was.

Having several dozen viewings under my belt, a now much-expanded library of life-enhancing self-development books (*life-enhancing* sounds like an upgrade of a couple of yellow bricks further along the *self-development* journey than *self-help*), and being well on my way along the path to changing my mind about my life, I had a very different listening of Dorothy's adventures in Oz. This time, at the end of the film when Dorothy woke up back in Kansas, I was not disheartened but heart-filled. Dorothy's whole life lay before her now because of her experiences in Oz and the wisdom she could now access.

It took the events of Dorothy's journey through Oz to reassemble the aspects of her character—her mental (brain), emotional (heart), intellectual (courage), physical (human), and spiritual (Divine) bodies—into alignment with the frequency of listening that was necessary for her to hear the wisdom and profound simplicity in Glinda's guidance. Dorothy had always had the power within her to go home, to claim her mastery, to fully realize her highest potential. However, to do so in a sustainable way, she had to start from the beginning and retrain herself to be conscious and intentional with each step along her path, to be present and pay attention to the signs along the way, and to appreciate the opportunity to remember who she was as a powerful force—a tornado of creative potential. Dorothy's adventures through Oz, much like her life in Kansas, didn't happen *to* her; they happened *for* her.

Later that evening, while lying in bed, I reflected on those earlier nights so long ago when I spent what seemed like hours promising myself that if being an adult meant I had to surrender my over-the-rainbow childlike wonder, I wanted nothing to do with it. This night, however, I saw how I didn't have to surrender anything except my limited thinking and beliefs that my life was something I had to survive. Oz isn't some place far, far away; it's a way of being, a way of believing; it's a journey to reclaiming ourselves that is best achieved when we start at the beginning.

CHAPTER ONE ACTION POINTS

One, Two, and Three

1) PRACTICE COMMON COURTESY AND BASIC MANNERS. Implementing "Thank you" and "Please" as habitual expressions of appreciation isn't about being polite or a good person, though it sure doesn't hurt. Rather, it is all about becoming conscious of managing ourselves into a constant state of *expanded* appreciation, understanding how appreciation is one of the quickest ways to raise our "feel good" vibration. The payoff is instant and very much self-serving, as it gives us direct access to a thriving experience of ourself, our life, and thus our humanity. In this, we see how the action of reclaiming our practice of appreciation is a first step in reclaiming our humanity.

While you're at it, why not supersize your experience by making eye contact during each "please" and "thank you." Eye contact is one of the art forms of humanity we have misplaced in our culture, yet it is one of the most effective and immediate ways to connect with each other. "Please" give it a try, and "thank you" for getting into action.

2) PAY ATTENTION TO THE BASIC SIGNS. One way to get in the practice of paying attention to the less-obvious signs the Universe is offering is to take note of the obvious signs right in front of us—literally. For example, how about becoming conscious and intentional of making complete stops at stop signs (and stoplights). I know; I can hear you. What the hell does stopping at a stop sign have to do with reclaiming our humanity? A reminder: If we can't even follow basic, obvious guidance, posted on physical tangible signs, how on earth will we follow the more subtle signs and guidance of our internal intuitive GPS? (More on that later.) The habit of making full stops at stop signs is a simple yet profound way of retraining ourselves into the practice of looking for, paying attention to, and honoring road signs, whether they be literal or figurative. So much of the chaos in the world is not a surprise given how many people are checked-out and unconscious to physical and intuitive signs while navigating basic daily life. Let's get back on track by retraining ourselves to follow the obvious signs posted around us, which are intended to keep us safe and lead us successfully to our destinations. This practice will assist us in developing a keener awareness of the obvious signs that have always been present, as well as becoming sensitive to the more subtle signs not so easily spotted with the human eye. In this, we also reduce the opportunities for being sideswiped because we were checked-out. Reclaiming our humanity requires we be present in our own journey, ready and willing to follow the signs along the path, all of which are in place to keep us on course.

Extra Credit: Get back in the practice of using your turn signals when making a change of direction or shifting lanes. Letting people in on your intentions helps them to help you move more safely in achieving your intention. Some of my clients have argued against the use of turn signals, claiming that it's not their job to inform other people of their every move. Not using turn signals is their inner rebel's way of "sticking it to the man." I invite these clients to consider retiring their Rebel Without a Cause resistance and put that energy into something that contributes to the advancement of humanity. As over-simplified as it may sound, the communication skill set of a person is revealed by how they use their turn signals. We have a lot of fun with this conversation in my workshops. Okay, better put, I have a lot of fun with this conversation in my workshops.

3) FINE-TUNE YOUR ATTITUDE OF GRATITUDE. Appreciation changes how we experience our world and ourselves in the world, setting us up to attract more to appreciate. Start with the things to appreciate that are right in front of you, at your fingertips—like running water or, better yet, warm running water. Give thanks to the Universe and the city and county water department each time you turn on the faucet and receive hot water. Water is a First World luxury we take for granted on a planet where many people don't have access to drinkable water, let alone running hot water. Again, appreciating hot water is not about being a good person or being thankful for having something that lesser-blessed people do not. These are noble ideas but not what we're aiming for here. We give thanks of appreciation because, in doing so, we are connecting with and acknowledging a most abundant and generous Universe. In this, we are again holding ourselves accountable for respecting and honoring what we have and, by proxy, intending it for everyone. Nurturing our humanity is an inside job, starting at home and expanding outward.

Going one step further, if you have access to a washing machine and a dryer in your home, give thanks as you transfer each load from one to the other. I remind myself regularly how, in a past life, I had to drag baskets of laundry down to the riverside and beat my clothes on rocks to get the stains out. Today, I get to apply stain remover, push a button, and go for a latte while the machine does the work. A big heartfelt "thank you" to Jacob Christian Schaffer of Germany, credited with the 1767 design, and all those who followed in the development of the electric washer and dryer.

CHAPTER TWO

STRING TRAINING

Changing Our Mind About What Limits Us

-STRAIGHT TALK-

ONE DEFINITION OF INSANITY IS DOING the same thing over and over and expecting different results. If we want to create something different, we have to get off our big BUTS of limited thinking and do something different.

-TALK STORY-

There is a particular technique used for training elephants that I like to use as a metaphor for how our thoughts and beliefs can keep us from realizing and achieving our full potential.

In this training, one end of a rope is tied to a hind leg of the baby elephant, and the other end is tied to a stake in the ground. The length of the rope determines the perimeter in which the baby elephant is physically able to navigate. The baby elephant, not knowing any different than what it has experienced, learns to journey no further than the tug of the rope on its leg. That world within the length of rope becomes the baby elephant's reality.

As the elephant grows in mass and accepts the perimeter within which its reality exists, it never occurs to the elephant to explore beyond the borders of this limited world he has come to know. With this training established (and self-managed by the elephant's mind), the trainer never needs to change out the original rope for a stronger piece of rope or chain. Even though the adult elephant could now, with minimal effort, break free from what seems like a mere string compared to his massive size, because of his training and belief, a stronger length of restriction is not necessary. For it is the thoughts of the elephant, not the strength of the "string," that keep him within the borders dictated by the training.

In this metaphor, we are like that baby elephant coming into the world full of potential. The rules, beliefs, and restrictions that are put upon us, and which we come to claim as our truth, are a string of beliefs tied at one end to our heart and at the other end to our perceived limitations. When first investigating the origins of our training, we are often met with "Because I said so," or "That's the way it has always been," or even more confusing, "I don't know." As we grow into adulthood, many of the thoughts, beliefs, and facts we inherited, though altered and watered down a bit, become the reality of the world we have created for ourselves and the borders behind which we live out our lives.

The thoughts we have about what is possible, as informed by the beliefs we have inherited and own (much like the string), are only as strong as the "truth" we give them. Consider, then, that a belief is a thought that has been thought, accepted, and believed long enough to be experienced as truth. Yet if a belief is learned through repetitive thought, might it also be unlearned and replaced with a repeated new thought? And if the new thought is thought long and often enough, might it become a new belief, delivering us to a new truth, a new possibility, and a new world experience?

A delightfully absurd example of familial training around limited thinking is one of my top ten favorite films adapted from the novel *Cold Comfort Farm* by British author Stella Gibbons. In this story, a recently orphaned young woman finds herself living with a family of distant cousins. Eccentric and tragic, the family rallies around a traumatic event the grandmother experienced some seventy years earlier when she saw something nasty in the woodshed. Confined to her bedroom, the grandmother comes out one night a year for the annual "counting"—a family roll-call intended to assure everyone is in check and keeps their place in the family story—a gathering which always begins with the matriarch announcing, "I saw something nasty in the woodshed ..." Throughout the film, whenever a family member even slightly hints of breaking from the tribe story, reference is made to the grandmother's traumatic event, and everyone falls back into line until, having been inspired and encouraged by their orphaned cousin, who is not invested in the family story, they don't. The plot plays out to a delightful ending, and in the final scene during a wedding celebration of new beginnings, we are reminded how, throughout this whole story, we, ourselves, never find out what the nasty thing was the grandmother saw in the woodshed all those years ago. To top it off, none of the characters in the story ever knew either. When their orphaned outsider muse asks the grandmother what actually happened, what she saw, the grandmother admits she doesn't remember. Without the ties of their old story holding them hostage, the family members are free to branch off to create their new stories and new lives.

CHAPTER TWO ACTION POINTS

Four, Five, and Six

4) WHEN SOMETHING OR SOMEONE INSPIRES YOU, SAY SO. You never know how your acknowledgment can inform someone's awareness and inspire them to shift their perspective of Self. It's not to be nice or a good person or polite; it is so much more self-serving an art form than that. An authentic and Soul-felt acknowledgment can instantly change the direction of an interaction, course-correct it up, expand it out, and breathe life into what might otherwise be an awkward and labored experience akin to navigating birth without an epidural.

5) GET EXCITED ABOUT SOMETHING–ANYTHING. *What* you are excited about is irrelevant to *that* you are excited about something. The energy of being excited keeps us engaged, motivated, curious, and forward-focused. And it feels good, so much better than feeling disconnected, unmotivated, bored, and stagnant.

6) CLEAN YOUR NOS. This action is short and sweet. Get used to saying No like you mean it. Nothing is more confusing to people than a wishy-washy No. If you are not available or interested in saying an authentic Yes to something, then by all means, offer a respectful, clear, and clean "No ... thank you."

CHAPTER THREE

AND THE OSCAR GOES TO ...

-STRAIGHT TALK-

NAVIGATING OUR PATH OF AT-ONE-MENT CAN be an obstacle course, awkward and clunky at first, as we trip, stumble, and fall like a toddler in the early journey of discovering balance. The key is to keep getting up and get back to it. Part of mastering the journey with grace is allowing ourselves to get it "wrong" as part of getting it "RIGHT." Each step along the way offers a lesson, an insight, and an opportunity.

-TALK STORY-

As a stage director, I invite my cast members to come to the first rehearsal bringing everything they know about life, all the tools they have developed as an actor, AND a willingness to explore the unknown. The relief the actors feel when the pressure is off to "get it right" from the first rehearsal creates a clearing for exploration and discovery. That's what rehearsals are for: to explore and play with as many options as we can imagine, harvesting golden nuggets along the way as we uncover creative genius. It's called a play for a reason.

Likewise, in the theatre of life, the path to genius is laden with obstacles challenging what we already know and accept as possible, while inviting us to move through our limited thinking to explore our untapped potential. The sense of imbalance and loss of control while exploring the unknown can be confronting and uncomfortable. Initially, we feel like Bambi walking on ice for the first time, legs flailing and sliding in every direction as we awkwardly acclimate to our new environment and relationship with balance.

I can remember being enthralled with the annual Academy Awards show well before my teens. Something about the excitement of movies, the parade of Hollywood royalty, and the celebration of storytelling captivated me. To this day, from the red carpet to the last words of the acceptance speech for Best Picture, I am off the grid. I joke with friends and family that the Oscars, for me, are the equivalent of an audience with the pope. I have no problem establishing and enforcing personal boundaries on Academy Awards night. From six to ten p.m., "I have no friends."

It is not every year I have the time or the desire to invest in going to the movie theaters and seeing all of the films nominated for Best Picture. Now, with the more recent practice of nominating nine to eleven films as opposed to the traditional five, it is even more of an effort to do so. However, 2017 was a terrific year for movies, and I was eager, intentional, and even obsessed with seeing all of the nine films nominated for the top honor.

As is the case throughout history, art finds a way of expanding its presence and influence during darker economic, political, and culturally challenging times, inspiring us to wake up, pay attention, and see things through a different set of lenses. Given our recent and current challenges, I figured Hollywood might have a bumper crop of films from which to select. I did see all nine films nominated for Best Picture, and I did see them on the big screen in movie theaters (appeasing my empathic and introverted personality by attending as many weekday matinee and evening showings as possible). None of the films disappointed me. I was so inspired, entertained, and motivated by each movie that I saw two of them twice and one three times. It was awesome.

One evening after seeing *The Phantom Thread*, one of the more absurd and curious movies, I took myself out for dinner so I could sit quietly and contemplate the complexity of the plot and character relationships. The small pub I selected for my post-Oscar-nominated-film-viewing fine dining experience was having a slow night, so there wasn't much activity to distract me from the serious business of processing. After ordering a veggie burger with a side of onion rings and a bottle of cider, I settled in for a period of reflection. (If you saw the film, you will appreciate the reasoning behind my having ordered the veggie burger **without** mushrooms.)

Three bites into my burger, I sensed someone coming up from behind me. Thinking it was the waiter checking in to see if the meal was to my liking, I looked up, intending to offer him a satiated smile. However, my eyes were met instead by a gentleman dressed in baggy clothes and a knitted ski hat, holding what I guessed to be his one-too-many bottles of beer. His eyes were glazed over, his stance a little waving, and his lips most likely heading toward the deep end of numb. He inquired if he might take a seat and join me for a minute. After scanning his vibe and arriving at an "all-clear" vetting result, I offered the universal hand gesture for "be my guest." Given the film I had just seen, it seemed absurdly appropriate this character would make his way to my table, enhancing my life as art, art as my life experience.

I would like to write word-for-word the conversation he believed he was having with me; however, being more of a monologue, it soon became obvious to me that my part was to serve as a witness rather than as a contributor. As noble as it would be to claim I had chosen to see and experience this man as a child of God rather than a drunken nuisance, it was my enjoyment of the award-winning onion rings and the mouth-watering veggie burger, rendering me unable to speak without a mouth full of food, which anchored my availability to engage in this one-sided encounter.

In my mind, I heard my "follow-your-six-sensory-training" inner voice telling me, "Pay attention. There is something here for you." Either that, or it was the cider kicking in. In any case, I listened through the slurred speech and the stream of (un)consciousness. I really had no idea what this guy's point was or where his short-bus-to-crazy-town was headed, but I was fast coming up on my last onion ring and would soon be running out of motivation to sustain interest.

Suddenly, just as I was taking the final bite of my burger, my dinner mate's mouth regained the motor skills of articulation as he stumbled through a request to, "Promise ... me ... something. Promise me ... something," to which I nodded my head in time with my chewing. Then, as if backlit with gold light and under-scored by harp music, he said very intentionally, "Promise me you will allow yourself to be awkwardly ... awesome."

(Silence, chew, pause, gulp.)

"Absolutely," I assured him, thinking to myself, "Where the heck did THAT come from?!"

Just then, the waiter came to the table to check in, this time to see if I needed any help with my tablemate situation. I gave him a nonverbal thumbs-up and asked for my check. Returning with a new laser-focused listening to my drunk guest, I knew this whole experience was Divinely guided and I was in the presence of a messenger with a profound instruction. This event wasn't my first time navigating a Divine encounter, and the request for a promise to be "awkwardly awesome" was not wasted on me.

I paid my check and tipped the waiter, and as I stood up from the table, my dinner guest rose to meet me with outstretched arms and a request for a hug. Without hesitation, I wrapped my arms around him in a hearty embrace, an expression of gratitude for our blessed encounter. I thanked him, wished him well, and headed out the door, smiling and musing to myself about my Divine encounter.

Walking to my car, the sobering effects of the cold winter night air hitting my face brought my thoughts back to the movie I had just seen. In that moment, the complexity of the absurd and curious plot and character relationships somehow paled in comparison to this most recent Divinely awkward and awesome experience.

I laughed and said, "And the Oscar for Best Picture goes to 'My Dinner with an 80 Proof Angel.'"

CHAPTER THREE ACTION POINTS

Seven, Eight, and Nine

7) CONSIDER THAT EVERYONE WHO CROSSES YOUR PATH COULD BE AN ANGEL WITH A MESSAGE. Angels can take on many forms (not all of them have wings) and show up in the most unlikely of places (you can count on that.) So we have to be at the ready with our willingness to be present, to listen, to receive, and to appreciate. Our life experience becomes enriched when we expect the unexpected and are willing to dance with it when it shows up.

8) DEVELOP YOUR VIBE SCANNING SKILLS. Our physical eyes rarely tell us the truth about what we are looking at, and our mind is navigating our eyes through the filters of emotions informed by our past experiences. What may look to us like one thing may be something else entirely. Training ourselves to check in with our gut feeling and doing what I call a vibe-check gives us a more accurate read on the situation.

9) ALLOW YOURSELF TO BE AWKWARDLY ... AWESOME. Get curious about what being awesome looks and feels like for you. You can count on this being an awkward exploration at first because you'll be navigating unfamiliar and uncomfortable territory. But what the heck, the worst that can happen is you discover something new about yourself and have Divine encounters along the way. The best that can happen is you start living your life with a "How good can I stand it?" attitude. Now that's pretty awesome.

PART TWO
SHIFTING THE
PARADIGM

CHAPTER FOUR

BUTTON, BUTTON, WHO'S GOT THE BUTTON?

Rewiring Our Emotional Access Panel

-STRAIGHT TALK-

People may push your buttons, but remember ... you installed them.

-TALK STORY-

Getting our emotional buttons pushed can be a jarring and disarming shock to the system, leaving us feeling sucker-punched and triggering any number of reactions along an expansive scale of emotions. These moments remind us of how, no matter what we know, what we do, and who we Be, we are not exempt from being accountable for managing our human emotional experience. Only when we have taken responsibility for how these buttons trigger and influence our toxic emotional reactions do we develop the ability to rewire and reprogram them to inform healthy emotional responses.

Rewiring our emotional button panel requires that we rewrite our story about each button, the people who push those buttons, and our willingness to reconsider why our buttons are available to be pushed. If we want to create something different, we have to do something different, which requires, first and foremost, that we choose to intend something different.

We cannot change the facts of our past; what has happened cannot be un-happened. So, that's the end of that. However, we can change our story about the facts, rewriting them to support a healthier, thriving version of how the data of the past informs our present and calls forth the potential of our future. I like to call this "Spinning fear into Love and living a thriving life."

Some may say this is a form of denial. To that, I say, "Absolutely!" Hey, we're always in denial of something: We are either denying our health or denying disease; we are either denying wealth or denying poverty; we are either denying Love or denying not-Love, etc. So, if we're always denying something, why not do it consciously and intentionally in favor of our health and wellness (and the highest potential of our humanity)? This choice is not complicated; however, it will take everything you have to shift, claim, and sustain the rewired, rewritten, and reprogrammed version of yourself and your buttons.

I had one of my Red Alarm buttons pushed one day in particular when I received a text message from my older brother, informing me that, "... we need to powwow about our *dear* mother." In that one sentence, a life history grounded in crossed wires and blown circuits launched a tsunami of emotions rushing to the forefront of my mind, triggering every cell of my body to kick into Code Red fight or flight mode.

Our mother, who had been navigating the tipping point of her end-of-life experience, was no longer capable of living alone in her home and not yet willing to surrender her now-compromised independence. In addition, our younger sister (having been the primary companion and caretaker for our mother) had recently been placed on a kidney/heart donor recipient list following decades of health issues and was no longer able to facilitate the daily demands of our mother's needs while she waited for a donor match, transplant surgery, and a lengthy recovery process. A heartbreaking situation with confronting details to address, the time had come for us to face reality and take action.

These facts of our mother's status came as no surprise, as she had been showing signs of physical decline, emotional instability, and more recently, stints with memory lapses. The added facts of our sister's medical situation, however, required an entirely distinct focus and set of action points. Understanding all of this in theory was one thing; addressing all of this in real time was quite another. We would have to move forward swiftly and efficiently if we were going to be effective in our efforts. Our mother and younger sister were a codependent duo with their own set of rules and immovable boundaries established around the lifestyle they had created together. My mother was Big Edie to my sister's Little Edie, and any actions we took would offset the balance of what I had come to reference as their adaptation of the mother/daughter relationship in *Grey Gardens*.

The emotional and physical reaction I had to the text I received from my older brother was not in response to the facts of our mother's and sister's health, but rather a reaction to the often-challenging relationship my brother and I navigated as influenced by our family history. To be successful in our efforts, I would have to find a way to work with my brother, whom I love with all my heart, yet whose intellect, emotionality, and personality I had never been able to engage with in any sense of safety, trust, or confidence.

Having spent most of my childhood and much of my adult life navigating the slings and arrows launched between my mother and brother, two equally matched opponents, I found myself more times than not caught in the crossfire of their disfavor and, at times, deep-seated detestation of each other. It was many years and a lot of practice before I would master the art of dodging their emotional sharpshooting.

As is the case with many parent/child personality conflicts, my mother and older brother had yet to connect the dots that would reveal how their strained relationship was grounded in their being more alike than not. I found this oversight on their part to be absurdly humorous, given how our mother had been an RN for thirty years and had a doctorate in public health and wellness. And my brother, having majored in psychology in college, fancied himself an expert on human behavior. They were masterful at pushing each other's buttons because of their similarities but would rather chew off their right arms than ever admit it to themselves or anyone else.

One of my favorite sayings regarding getting our buttons pushed goes something like, "People may push your buttons, but remember, you installed them." This statement always triggers a groan from my clients, followed by a laugh of uncomfortable recognition. Saying this to a client in setting up for a breakthrough in consciousness is one thing—bringing it up casually during a family gathering could have gotten me knocked unconscious. With our pending "powwow," the time had come and the opportunity had presented itself for me to take the steps necessary to close the gap between my training in facilitating paradigm shifts for clients and my position as enabling peacekeeper in the family dynamic.

I knew if I wanted to create something different in my experience of my older brother, I would have to do something different in how I related to him. And if I wanted to relate differently to *him*, I would first need to relate differently to *myself.*

I spent some time in walking meditation, asking myself who I could Be with my brother, the Being of which could change everything. What I got was clear, to the point, and totally doable: "Hold the vibration of Love, listen in Love, and speak with Love." This way of showing up was not a new concept for me, given that this is how I have been trained and practiced in showing up for my clients, workshops, and classes. However, this was my brother: We had a history, we had filters. I had a story about him; he had a story about me. I had a story about who he is for me; he had a story about who I am for him. I knew, if I was going to show up differently, I was going to have to hold myself accountable for managing my triggers and self-installed buttons. So, I closed the door on my emotional panel of buttons and slapped a lock on it.

I was ready; I had found my footing. I sent my brother a text to confirm a time for us to chat the following day, knowing that I had twenty-four hours to do a major overhaul in the rewriting of my story, rewiring of our story, and reprogramming of our family dynamic. At the confirmed time, I cleared my mind, grounded myself with a few deep breaths, chose Love, and dialed my brother's phone number. Our conversation lasted about twenty minutes, and in that short time, we were able to address the facts of our mother's situation without emotional charge, consider our options, identify which family member's skill set was best suited for taking the lead on each issue, and establish a first-step action point plan. We also considered a couple of alternate backup options, understanding how the best-laid plans do not guarantee synergistic responses. We were in alignment, on the same page, and focused in the same direction.

At this point in our conversation, I detected a slight shift in my brother's tone, a shift I recognized as the tendrils of manipulation. A shift which, in the past, triggered the onset of my feeling depleted of life-force, submitting to the will of my brother, and falling victim to his need for intellectual and emotional domination. (I would later come to identify his behavior as gaslighting.) However, this time, something was different. Since I had been consciously and intentionally conducting myself in the vibration of Love from the onset of the conversation, I was grounded and anchored. In the Love I had been holding and sustaining, his access to my buttons had been denied.

Being in the listening of Love, I heard and experienced this shift in my brother's tone differently. In that moment, I considered for the first time how my brother was navigating his own fear: the fear that our younger sister, with all of her ailments, might not make it through all of this alive. He was in that moment a vulnerable and frightened child who, no matter how smart he was, how successful he was, how many millions of dollars he had, found himself feeling powerless in his ability to save his little sister's life. And hearing him differently, I responded differently. And it was my response that changed the dynamic of our relationship.

I knew if we were going to find the clarity and peace necessary to support us through this process, we would have to rewire this dance of our family dynamic on the spot in real time. One of us had to shift the paradigm of our family dynamic, break the cycle, relinquish our wounded-child story, and rewrite our potential in this present moment. I could no longer continue enabling his version of me as the naive little brother, the goody-two-shoes, to be dismissed as delusional to the workings of the "real world." At the same time, I would need to remove the labels I had assigned to him as the "bad seed" of the family, a self-appointed savior, and nemesis to our mother. If our efforts would be successful, we had to find our way to the healed adult version of ourselves.

In the flash of a moment, tucked within the rapid-fire process I was navigating, I recalled a distinction of child development discussed in Alice Miller's book *The Drama of the Gifted Child: The Search for the True Self.* I had read the book maybe three months earlier, so the topic was fresh in my mind. In the book, Alice Miller makes the point of how the healed adult stands on the foundation of the healed inner child. If the inner child remains wounded, the wounds are carried as truths into adulthood. Reading that book, which I highly recommend, I recalled connecting dots around how both our mother and father were wounded children playing the roles of adults. And they were, therefore, raising wounded children. We weren't unique in this. Most adults see and experience the world informed by their filters—filters established from traumatic defining moments encountered during their childhood years.

My wounded inner child in check, I called upon my healed inner child to hold me steady as I stepped up to offer to my brother the healed-adult version of myself, a version of myself I was still developing and the version of myself he had not yet experienced. I would offer this in the form of Loving him, believing in him, and supporting him. All of this would include some tough-love straight talk. So, I took a deep breath, double-checked the lock on the door of my emotional buttons, stepped out of my status as little brother, and introduced him to my new role in our relationship.

Having chosen to respond in Love rather than react in anger, I trusted the appropriate words would come to me. From this closed-panel positioning, I was able to call my brother out and up on his behavioral track record. "I have to say something that you are not going to like, but it has to be addressed if we are going to be effective in our efforts." In Love, I was able to share with my brother my experience of his toxic behavior patterns when he was navigating depression and substance abuse. How his history of being emotionally unreliable and self-destructive had created a distrust of him among the family.

I was then inspired to acknowledge his intellectual strengths, his mastery of business and legal issues, and his potential for effective leadership. All of these were his power tools. However, depending on his mental and emotional clarity, these same tools could also be weapons of mass destruction. "With one email or phone call, you could destroy all of our efforts." If he was going to step up and be effective in *his* efforts, he was going to have to manage himself into alignment with being conscious in his actions for the benefit of all concerned, or he was going to have to self-select out of any leadership position. And I was going to hold myself accountable for holding him accountable for that.

There was a long silence from my brother at his end of the connection. I waited for him to speak next, understanding I had redefined our relationship, and he would either react with an attack or respond with something new. And when he did speak, there was a profound sense of calm and a humbled strength in his tone. "Thank you for saying that. It needed to be said." By withholding access to my emotional buttons, I was able to engage him without pushing his buttons. We then reviewed the action points we planned to implement, agreed to check in with an update, and said "I love you" to wrap up our deliberation.

In that moment, we created access to new possibilities. I had no idea how things would play out; I had no expectations, no attachments, and no delusions of grandeur about any of it. By proxy, representing both of us, I would take the journey one day, one step, and one breath at a time. I would navigate each moment with a refined intention, a keener listening, and a willingness to explore a new potential—one grounded in Love, navigated with Love, and informed by Love.

Does my older brother still try to push my buttons? Sure. He wouldn't be an older brother if he didn't. However, those buttons have become a lot more difficult for him to find and push. When he does, I hold myself accountable for remembering that I installed them, and I control how I react or respond when triggered. It has taken a lot of practice—I won't water down that reality. However, with practice, his hits-to-misses ratio has shifted considerably. And that has made all the difference … for both of us.

CHAPTER FOUR ACTION POINTS

Ten, Eleven, and Twelve

10) SHIFT YOUR INTENTION. We see what we project onto any experience. If we want to see differently, we have to project differently. Our past-as-the-truth creates an *already-always-listening* in which we believe we know exactly how an experience will progress. Be willing to create a different experience of someone by shifting your intention about what is possible with the person. When we bring Love to any situation, we will find the Love in that situation. Be more interested in the Love than in being right. The people may still behave the way they always have; however, someone has to show up differently first to create the opportunity for change. Be willing to give up having to be right about how things always go.

11) SHIFT YOUR LISTENING. We hear what we project onto any experience. If we want to hear differently, we have to listen differently. Our past-as-the-truth creates an *already-always-listening* in which we believe we already know how an experience will play out. Be willing to have someone show up differently by shifting your intention about what is possible with the person.

When we project Love onto any situation, we will find the Love in that situation. Be more interested in listening through Love than in being right. People may still say what they have always said; however, someone has to show up willing to hear something differently first to create the opportunity for a different experience. If you have to be right about something, be right about that.

12) SHIFT YOUR POTENTIAL. We create what we project onto any experience. If we want to create a different experience, we have to project the potential for a different possibility. Our past-as-the-truth creates an *already-always-listening* in which we believe we know how an experience will turn out. Be willing to create a different experience by shifting your intention about what is possible in any given situation. When we project Love onto any situation, standing in the potential to create something different, we make room for something we've never allowed ourselves to consider before. Be more interested in creating something new than in perpetuating something old.

CHAPTER FIVE

I DON'T THINK SO!

Saying No to Energy Suckers

-STRAIGHT TALK-

NOBODY TAKES ANYTHING FROM US THAT we do not give to them, consciously or unconsciously.

-TALK STORY-

Energy suckers are people who, doubting their potential, feed on the energy of others rather than tapping into their own life-force. Because they believe they need to feed on the energy of others, they are always on the lookout for a source of life-force to hook up to. We're not interested in being someone's energy "juice box." So, we need to be conscious and intentional about being as unattractive as possible to energy vampires. Knowing how to read people's energy and having confidence in our ability to do so is a great foundation. However, it doesn't hurt to have a little extra backup support. First, just as with the vampires in horror movies, the number one rule for energy vampires is: They have to be invited into your home to gain access. No Invite = Access Denied. Second rule: Like vampires, the energy sucker cannot see his/her reflection in a mirror. If you are not available to engage, you cannot be a source of reflection (and oh, how the energy sucker longs to gaze upon his/her reflection).

Years ago, I was facilitating a nine-week class series called *Your Heart's Desire, Creating the Life You Really Want to Live,* created and developed by my friend and colleague Sonia Choquette. I love facilitating these classes, feeling honored and blessed to hold space for the participants as each one takes ownership of their life and breaks through the glass ceiling of their creative potential. In this particular group of participants was a first-time client who had never worked with me before and had not yet become acquainted with my style of facilitating. In the first session, when it came her turn to introduce herself to the group of fellow participants, she shared about having studied with a number of gurus and—looking directly at me—announced her disappointment in not yet having found her purpose; she was once again in the market for a new guru. She ended her share with the tagline, "... and *you* might just be *my* new guru."

I understood how she was trying to make an impression on the class and a connection with me. However, as well-intended as her invitation may have been, the weight and intensity of her comment was more than a bit creepy (picture Gollum from *The Lord of the Rings* trilogy) and sent chills down my spine, triggering warning buttons on my emotional button panel. I couldn't tell if the participant intended to praise me by appealing to my ego or prey on me by appealing to my recovering fixer/pleaser/caretaker. Either way, I was not available or interested in having anyone latch on to me and tap into my life-force.

My formal training as a professional intuitive had prepared me for such encounters. As a spiritual teacher and change facilitator, it was imperative that I be unavailable (even unattractive) to potential Energy Suckers, who tend to take facilitators and entire classes hostage with their need to feed on external sources.

To maintain integrity for myself, the class, and the participant, I needed to establish a clear boundary in that moment, on the spot. Positioning myself in the frequency of Love, I looked directly into her guru-hungry eyes and announced very clearly and assertively, "Probably not." (There was a collective breathless pause, during which you could have heard a mosquito scratch his bum.)

"I don't want you to engage me as your guru. I want you to be your own guru. You're looking for someone to validate you and ultimately blame for your failures. I want you to claim your success. And you will never accomplish that if you continue to surrender your personal power over to an external guru."

I understood how I would not be effective as a facilitator if I encouraged and enabled a "guru" relationship with this participant, or any of the participants enrolled in the class, or any class, for that matter. Non-attachment is key to being an effective facilitator/coach in any situation. I understood it was not my place, nor was it appropriate for me to engage in any energetic relationship that might encourage an unhealthy attachment, which often leads to codependency and enabling. It's not that I don't care; I'm just very clear of the fine line between *caring* for someone's story and *carrying* someone's story.

I considered how this client might choose not to return for the next session or any of the remaining sessions of the class series. As profound and loving as the guidance was, there were a number of interpretations she could have optioned to support her own story. Yet when she did show up for the next session, she looked different, something had shifted, and she had warrior energy stirring within her. She had heard the stand I had taken for her and had taken the first steps in finding her new guru, her inner guru. She was ready to claim her success, no blaming about it.

Taking a stand for myself, I knew I was also taking a stand for this client's potential and, by proxy, the potential of everyone in the class as individuals and as a collective.

This experience was a reminder to never surrender our personal power over to anyone else. Not so much to protect ourselves from energy predators, though that is part of it, but rather to hold ourselves accountable for managing ourselves in our potential. No one else can do this work for us, claim our personal power for us, or sustain our personal power for us. It's an inside job.

No matter how tempting it is, and the temptation is overwhelming at times, it is never appropriate for our individual or collective well-being to surrender our power over to an authority figure—whether political, religious, employer, friend, or family. A powerful teacher/leader of integrity will never ask us to surrender our personal power over to the altar of their ego. Instead, the empowering teacher/leader of integrity will stand in the fire with us—never for us—with non-attachment, holding us accountable for claiming, owning, and sustaining our highest potential fully-realized.

During a meditation on this topic, I was visiting with the Master Teachers and inquired what they wanted us to know about their teachings that we were not yet clear on, that which our getting clear on would change everything.

"We were not looking to create followers. We were, however, intending to manifest colleagues."

CHAPTER FIVE ACTION POINTS

Thirteen, Fourteen, and Fifteen

13) WHEN SOMEONE TELLS YOU WHO THEY ARE, BELIEVE THEM. As empathic beings, we are all sensitive to the energetic offering of the people we encounter. It's how we're wired. So, it would make sense to pay attention not only to the words people use and the actions they present but also to the vibrational frequency of the energy each projects. On average, most people's words, actions, and energetic offerings do not match. This contradiction can be confusing, leaving us with an unsettling feeling about someone who sounds great in words or whose actions are attractive, when the more reliable broadcast of who they are is their energetic offering. In most cases, they're not even aware they have an energetic offering, making this an even more authentic and accurate informant of their character. If the vibe is "off-putting," we can take it as a red flag of caution. Notice how I said caution, not fear. We want to be accountable for our listening (energy read) of someone—and not project our own energetic offering onto the other person, thus getting a reading of our own vibe being mirrored back to us. Fear can be a projection-reflection. Caution is being conscious about the what-is of any situation.

14) TRUST YOUR VIBRATIONAL RED FLAGS. In a pocket-sized notebook, keep a record of your energy (intuitive) hits. This writing is more about creating a database of evidence to support the idea that the whole energy thing is real and to support you in building your confidence in proving to yourself how you are already skilled at being tuned-in to vibes.

15) WEAR ENERGY GARLIC. Your greatest power tool against energy suckers is your unwillingness to engage. Not out of fear, remember, but out of recognition. The last thing an energy sucker wants to do is hang out with people who've "got their number." Awareness is to the energy sucker like garlic is to the vampire. Similarly, your unwillingness to engage is to the life-force feeder like water is to the Wicked Witch of the West … and we all know how *that* witch went down.

CHAPTER SIX

UP ON YOUR TOES WITH YOUR ARMS IN THE AIR

"Wybieramy sie na lody!"

-STRAIGHT TALK-

WITH AN INFINITE NUMBER OF POSSIBILITIES to choose from, what are you choosing to go with?!

On some level, we've accepted the "reality" that life is hard, bad things happen to good people, and surviving through life is the best we can expect.

On some level, we also believe the truth that life is awesome, good things happen to all people, and thriving through life is our birthright.

-TALK STORY-

On a recent trip to Europe, I was blessed to have participated in a day-long private group tour of Warsaw, Poland, exploring this historic city with our wonderful (and knowledgeable and equally passionate) guide, Iolanta. A couple of hours into our adventure, we were walking along a path through the old Jewish Ghetto, now a series of refurbished apartment buildings, when a mother and three children ages five to ten abruptly came out of one of the first-floor units and headed in our direction.

The mother was focused and intent on her mission, no-nonsense in her manner, and attentive to her three charges. In the perceived absence of a wedding band on either hand, my guess was she had found herself the sole caretaker of her little tribe. Her "mom" uniform consisted of bleached blond hair pulled back in two braids (revealing a half-inch of dark roots), a faded dark-blue spaghetti-strap camisole-style top, a pair of pink terry cloth shorts, and flip-flop sandals. Pushing a stroller stocked with a blanket and basics for their outing, she was followed by a shaggy-haired boy of about ten, a long-haired girl maybe a year younger, and a five-year-old towheaded boy, all dressed in a mix-and-match selection of play clothes.

The mother and two oldest children passed by us with the chaos that comes with herding children at a determined pace. The littlest of the three children was the last of the clan to pass by, and as he did, he turned to us. Rolling up onto his tiptoes and raising his arms in the air (appearing as if he might just leap out of his body), with a wide-eyed angelic expression and animated unapologetic enthusiasm, he announced to our guide at the top of his voice, "Wybieramy sie na lody!"

Iolanta (the only Polish-speaking member of our group) leaned down toward the boy and, matching his enthusiasm, rejoiced along with him in their native language.

With this, the little boy then turned and rushed to catch up with his family. Iolanta, with a twinkle in her eye and as much of a smile as her Polish culture would allow (and maybe just a little more), translated the child's announcement for us: "We're going for ice cream!"

Iolanta then translated her exchange with the boy, informing us she had acknowledged and celebrated his adventure, then had instructed him to catch up with his family, and, "Give your mama a **big** hug."

That was it. I was a pile of Jell-O. This little ambassador of Love had instantly gotten me out of my head, which had been processing the intense history lesson I had been absorbing. I can only speak for myself; however, I imagine I was not the only member of our group whose heart flew wide open in contagious response to the boy's delight. I took a moment to manage the lump in my throat, holding back what would most definitely have been an unapologetic ugly-cry of overwhelmed inspiration.

Watching the boy pull up alongside his mother (and give her a *big* hug), I became aware for the first time that she had tattoos on both of her calves: Mickey Mouse on the left and Minnie Mouse on the right. My inner Disney child smiled, remembering that Magic is where we create it.

During the years of WWII, 85 percent of the city of Warsaw was destroyed in bombing attacks. The Jewish Ghetto had been a place of fear and chaos as, daily, residents were separated and transported to any one of a number of death camps. The Warsaw of today, much of which has been rebuilt from the rubble remaining from the war, is, after thirty-plus years under Communist rule, in the early stage of reinventing itself as a democracy.

However, that day, in that moment, through the eyes of childlike wonder, Warsaw, Poland, was the happiest place on Earth because "Wybieramy sie na lody!"

CHAPTER SIX ACTION POINTS

Sixteen, Seventeen, and Eighteen

16) LEARN SOMETHING NEW ABOUT SOMEONE, SOMEPLACE, OR SOME-THING. The world is not as big as it used to be, and more and more, we are coming to see how we are all connected, whether by the internet, social media, our beliefs, or our humanity. At our human core, we all want the same things. At our Soul core, we are all at One with each other. Our Atonement, At-One-Ment, is non-negotiable, non-dismissive, all-inclusive. The more we reach out to understand each other, the more we understand how we are reaching from the same heart place for the same heart things.

17) BE WILLING TO BE INSPIRED OUT OF YOUR MIND. So much of our time, energy, and focus is given to, and exhausted by, what we think we need to get "done" in "order to" ... (fill in the blank). We can be so distracted by our past (chewing gum for the mind) and worried about our future (which, by the way, doesn't exist yet) that we aren't even present in the present, as a present. If we allow ourselves to be inspired by the "little" blessings offered up to us every day, we learn to move through our day Woke, and we won't need so many uncomfortable sledgehammer wake-up calls.

18) GO FOR ICE CREAM. Whether metaphorically or literally, go for what feeds your Spirit. Everyone loves what feeds their Spirit, whether it's music, dance, art, or ice cream (all of which are languages without borders). What feeds our individual Spirit nurtures our collective Soul.

PART THREE
CLAIMING OUR POTENTIAL

CHAPTER SEVEN

ONE THING I KNOW FOR SURE

—STRAIGHT TALK—

IF I HAVE COME TO KNOW one thing for sure, it is this: We are all energetically connected as extensions and expressions of pure positive Source energy, the Source energy of everything. This energetic connection is infinite and eternal with no boundaries or disconnects. As we become more aware of and more practiced in remembering (re-membering, re-assembling) this eternal truth of who we are and our eternal connection within Source, we are better prepared and able to sustainably fuel our humanity with Love, in Love, as Love for the benefit of all concerned. Our remembrance intact, we see and experience the Oneness of ourselves, the world, and each other more accurately and authentically. We make different choices, take different actions, and create different results as we navigate our humanity from a Source awareness perspective. In our At-One-Ment, we gain unobstructed access to claiming and sustaining our humanity at its highest potential fully-realized.

AT THIS JUNCTURE IN THE PROCESS of reclaiming our humanity, we reach the tipping point in the paradigm shift of our efforts. As referenced in the *How the Book Works* portion of the Introduction, the first six chapters were an invitation to consider how we can consciously and intentionally course-correct our participation into alignment with the healed version of our individual humanity. The following six chapters are a guideline for how we may effectively participate in aligning ourselves with the broader expression of our thriving collective humanity. You will find this shift reflected in the tone of the remaining Straight Talk, Talk Story, and Action Points— designed to engage you in opening your heart and your mind to an expanded awareness and mastery of our At-One-Ment and our collective potential.

-TALK STORY-

Imagine the vast ocean as Source; imagine the waves as extensions of Source. The ocean is always the ocean, and sometimes the ocean expresses itself as waves—fanning over the surface of the beach and then withdrawing back into the vast Source from which it extended. The ebb and flow of the surf is the eternal dance of the sea, just as the ebb and flow of the Soul is the eternal dance of Source, always non-physical and sometimes expressed into physical.

The Master Teachers throughout human history have understood this distinction and are disciplined in navigating their physical (expression) experience from their Source (extension) awareness. The Master Teachers also know that being eternal, the Soul cannot be dismissed, displaced, or diminished and can never *not* be whole, complete, and Divine. It can, however, become coated with energetic pollutants, appearing distorted and diseased, yet, at its core, the Soul remains in its purest eternal form.

A distinction in *A Course In Miracles* suggests that the miracle does not bring something to the healing process but rather removes all things (in the form of limiting beliefs) that have obstructed the healing process. Much like a water molecule shedding accumulated layers of toxic buildup as it is put through the water purification process, once again revealing the core essence of its unalterable purity, so, too, does the Soul shed the layering buildup of toxic energy acquired during the human experience.

This Soul toxin-shedding process is programmed by Divine design to take place as the Soul, having completed its physical world experience, withdraws from the physical body. It releases all beliefs of disease and limitation navigated as an appropriate and profound part of its earthbound Soul Lesson and Soul Agreement agenda, as it is absorbed back into its eternal non-physical state.

We are as much connected and in this together as a humanity as we are all in this together and connected as expressions of Source, here in the physical world doing our Soul-part in support of the eternal expansion of Source. (That's an expansive conversation we'll save for a whole other book.) Our Souls choose a Soul Lesson curriculum to experience, and coordinate our parts and our partners with whom we will play out our Soul Agreements.

Using a theatre reference as an analogy, think of all of us as actors in a repertory theatre company of Souls. We have all been cast in various roles in a variety of productions to be performed in repertory. One night, in a musical, we could sing our way through our roles with me cast in the role of your father and you in the role of my daughter. In the next night's production, a farce, where you are cast in the role of the queen and me in the role of court jester, we enter and exit through a dozen slamming doors, catching each other in questionable states of undress. On the following night, in a comedy, we could be playing lovers, working together to navigate our mismatched families. And on the next night, in another production, a tragedy, you could be playing the role of my perpetrator, and I, playing the role of your victim, could die at your hands as the lights fade to black at the end of the first act. And so on.

In this analogy, we are all members of the same acting troupe playing various roles in various productions. We play our part in the plot of each production and give our best performance in each role. After the final curtain call, we withdraw to our dressing rooms and, while removing our costumes, wigs, and makeup, release the essence of the characters whose stories we just told. We retreat from their worlds, their journeys, and their thoughts, words, and actions. As actors, like Souls, we do not confuse ourselves with the roles we have played. We're storytellers; we take the journey of the play, further mastering our craft and discovering something new with each performance. When the show is over, we all go out for a post-show beer to celebrate a job well done. No longer the father/daughter, the queen/court jester, the lovers, the perpetrator/victim; we are players communing as one troupe.

Much like an actor playing a character in a live performance, the Soul, too, is playing a character in a *life* performance. Part of the actor's job is to have a big-picture understanding of their role and the evolution their character experiences as they navigate their journey of the scripted plot. However, to achieve an authentic performance, the actor must present the story as if the character he/she is portraying does not know the progression and the outcome of the plot. What the next scene holds for the character, though known by the actor, must remain unknown to that character for the play to work successfully. This knowing, too, can be said for the Soul.

Our Soul knows the big-picture plot line of our life. However, to achieve an authentic experience of our life-performance, we, the character—the physical expression of our Soul—can only know what is appropriate for us to know in any given moment in the real time of our performance. Because of this, our life can feel less like a scripted production and more like a never-ending improv of *Whose Line Is It Anyway?*

Using the Source-as-Ocean and the Soul-as-Actor analogies to help us wrap our minds around these expansive concepts, we position ourselves to bring our Source extension and Soul expression awareness to our physical world human experience. From this perspective, we see and experience each other more accurately, asking more appropriate questions about our lives, recognizing the eternal connection in each other, making more conscious and intentional choices about how we contribute to the greater good.

One thing I have come to know for sure is that we are eternally connected as extensions and expressions of pure positive Source energy, the energy that creates worlds. When we remember who we are in this eternal Love energy, we bring this remembrance, this re-membering, to the foundation of how we choose to navigate our human experience. Having claimed our birthright of Atonement, we create direct access to reclaiming our humanity at its fully-realized potential.

The largest investment of effort on our part in this stage of claiming our potential is in our willingness to consider who we are as extensions and expressions of pure positive Source energy. This willingness to remember is enough to launch us exponentially forward into our At-One-Ment and reclaim our humanity. Once we are sustainably willing, the re-membering falls into place naturally with the strength and grace of clarity.

CHAPTER SEVEN ACTION POINTS

Nineteen, Twenty, and Twenty-One

19) ASK THE AUTHENTIC CONSCIOUS QUESTION. Asking for clarity when we are frustrated about something and want to understand how to handle the situation or why the experience is happening, we will manifest an answer that is the closest match to the vibration from which we asked the question. So, if we ask a question from a place (a vibrational offering) of frustration, we can only hear (manifest) an answer that supports and matches the vibration of frustration. We can find some relief in this, in that we feel validated in our frustration, and for a while, we may be content. However, it is not long before we get frustrated again (or more so) and ask another question, which calls forth another answer of equal vibration … and so on. We get caught in a loop of one step forward, two steps back, a half-step forward, one step back, no step forward, one step back. And before long, we're only moving backward, further and further down the rabbit hole of despair. Of course, this is an unconscious process, for who in their right mind would consciously choose to remain stuck in a loop of frustration?

When we bring a conscious intention to our question and ask for clarity from the place of our At-One-Ment (from our intended healed humanity), we call forth an answer that guides us beyond the place from which we asked the question and into an answer beyond what we had previously known or considered possible. We are now moving one step forward and one step forward and one step forward. I always invite my clients to consider that, rather than asking, "Why is this happening *to* me?" ask instead, "Why is this happening *for* me?" In this one shift of perspective, we position ourselves out of alignment with the stuck victim and into alignment with the forward-moving warrior.

If we want to supersize our question and call forth a profound answer, we can ask, "What is *this* trying to show me, the seeing of which will change everything?" Then listen with a willingness to hear and see beyond what our current reality dictates as possible. This question doesn't just set us up to move forward; it sets us up to *launch* forward.

20) PRACTICE AN AUTHENTIC NAMASTE. Namaste (nä-mə-stä) is a sacred greeting announcing, "The Divine in me recognizes and honors the Divine in you." Accompanied with the hands in praying position and a slight bow of the head, this is a most beautiful Soul-to-Soul acknowledgment. To see the Soul in the person to whom we are extending the Namaste, we must first acknowledge the Soul that we are and offer the greeting from our

Soul (Self) awareness. "The whole, complete, and Divine in me recognizes and acknowledges the whole, complete, and Divine in you." In this, we are One in At-One-Ment with each other.

Few things are more disorienting (and disturbing) than a Soulless Namaste, or as I like to call it, Faux-maste. If you're going to offer or receive a Namaste, make it a conscious, intentional, authentic Soulful experience. Integrity is key.

21) BE THE CHANGE YOU WISH TO SEE IN THE WORLD. A key component to feeling stuck, or worse, helpless, is the unconscious practice of surrendering our power to external influences. Another loop we get stuck in is the "If *they* would only change, then I could … (fill in the blank)." As much as we would like to believe we would be happier, healthier, wealthier, etc., if only our spouse, children, co-workers, government, etc., would change, this isn't going to happen. What we are really saying is, "If only everyone else would behave the way I want and need them to behave, then I could be happy." That's just plain delusional and a complete cop-out. We cannot control other people or external events. We can, however, control how we choose to show up in our thoughts, words, and actions. In fact, how we are showing up is the *only* thing we can control. The sooner we get real about this, the better off we'll be and the more influential we will be in reclaiming our humanity. When we remember who we are as whole, complete, and Divine, we show up in the world as an asset rather than a liability, an inspiration for the change we desire.

CHAPTER EIGHT

THE RETROGRADE PHENOMENON

*Walking Through the Chaos with
the Strength of Grace*

-STRAIGHT TALK-

Shift happens. There is no way around it; the only way is through it. What determines the state of our well-being when we come out the other side is influenced and informed by who we choose to Be while walking through the shift storm.

-TALK STORY-

Several years ago, we found ourselves in the middle of a retrograde experience hailed as one of the most intense in

one hundred years. Enhanced by the already-chaotic cultural climate, it is no wonder we felt untethered in a magnified sense of vulnerability.

The rotation of the planets in our solar system around our Sun is a wonder of nature. Astrologists, scientists, and poets alike have been studying, documenting, and articulating this activity since astrologists, scientists, and poets first looked toward the heavens and got curious about what's going on up there. Any number of theories and studies, thoughts and beliefs, facts and mythologies exist about the workings of all those spinning celestial objects. However, bottom line, no matter which perspective we take or with which belief we resonate, the fact is: the Universe works the way it works, has always worked the way it works, and will most likely continue to work the way it works. It's the natural way of things.

The term "retrograde" in regard to our solar system suggests a redirection or backward movement. This perceived change in direction is just that—a perception—thanks to the discoveries of Copernicus. In the case of Mercury in retrograde, the planet Mercury does not actually reverse direction on its rotation around the Sun. This optical illusion is caused by the position of Mercury as it relates to Earth at a specific alignment. It's all about timing, positioning, and perspective: relativity.

The energetic influence of this planetary alignment does, however, have an energetic influence on the solar system, as is the case with all planetary alignments, at any time, in any formation. However, the duration of this particular retrograde alignment causes the particular energetic shift we experience on Earth. It is this distinct energetic "disruption" that we on Earth experience as imbalanced and out-of-sorts. The *appearance* of the retrograde effect may be an illusion; however, the *energetic* influence during these experiences is quite real. Whether we are consciously or unconsciously aware of being empathic to this energetic influence, we are affected by it. The more empathic we are, the more dramatic the experience. And the less grounded the empath, the more traumatic the experience.

One reason these fluxes in energy can cause such a deep sense of imbalance and chaos in our individual and collective experience is that humans don't like change and don't like to be inconvenienced. It could be said for most, if not all, natural phenomenon: It is only when humans are involved that a natural phenomenon is experienced as "negative" and deemed a natural disaster. If a tree falls in the woods, and no one is around for it to fall on, who is there to blame, and who is there to do the blaming?

Considering this, rather than butting heads with the natural order of things, might we be better served to manage ourselves in ways that have us going *with* the natural flow of things? This mindset shift doesn't mean life won't be intense, scary, or challenging. It does, however, mean we can set ourselves up to be prepared, have a plan, and navigate the path of least resistance more effectively and efficiently.

Growing up in Southern California, where the natural phenomenon of earthquakes and aftershocks were part of the reality of living seventeen miles from the San Andreas fault line, we learned to move (quite literally) with the natural way of things. The first quake was always the most dramatic because it would appear to come out of nowhere. Only if you had learned to recognize the warning signs (birds going silent, the frantic barking of dogs, an eerie stillness in the air) would you have the potential to make your way to the nearest doorway or dive under the sturdiest table before the first jolt or ripple of shock waves would roll from underfoot.

A mild to moderate quake, depending on the duration and intensity, could be like riding a stand-up roller coaster, rolling and jolting with nothing to hold on to that wasn't moving. As unnerving as the total (if only temporary) loss of control was, most quakes would trigger an adrenaline rush, leaving your eyes wide as saucers and you short of breath. If physical damage marked the event—a crack in the wall, a broken vase, or a tilted painting—you would have physical proof to justify your howler monkey screaming or slightly soiled undergarments.

The larger quakes, however, were another story all together. With these more destructive and potentially life-threatening quakes, things could, in a matter of seconds, advance to a full-on natural disaster. With these more intense quakes, or for that matter, any quake, a guaranteed and unpredictable number of aftershocks would vary in degree of intensity and regularity. It was this "not if, but when" uncertainty that caused much trauma. With the initial earthquake, you don't see it coming, and it catches you by surprise, kicking the fight-or-flight survival instinct into superhuman mode. With the unsettling and disorienting effects of potentially dozens of aftershocks eating away at your nerves, your nervous system can become so fatigued that the slightest sound or movement will induce a total meltdown. (It was four months after the Whittier quake of 1987 before I was able to sleep through the night without breaking out in a cold sweat of panic with the slightest disruption.)

Earthquakes, like retrogrades, are a natural phenomenon. A big difference, however, is that with an earthquake, or any natural disaster, there is a physical experience with physical effects. Being able to point to the physical damage helps justify and validate the trauma we are experiencing. In this, we are, to varying degrees, able to wrap our minds around the experience, find a way to make sense of it, and move on to the recovery and healing process.

Retrogrades, on the other hand, being a primarily energetic influence, are much more mysterious, with no tangible physical effects to point to for validation. In this, we can see the desire, if not the need, to point at and believe the illusion of the reversal of movement associated with a retrograde as the cause and evidence of our sense of imbalance. Unlike earthquakes, retrogrades are a steady, extended, and disorienting experience.

Unless we are conscious and intentional about how we manage ourselves, we can easily spin out of control with our emotions, thoughts, words, and actions. In this, we, ourselves, become the natural disaster, triggering a parade of aftershocks and leaving a trail of physical and emotional damage in our wake.

When we live in a geographical region known to be vulnerable to natural phenomena and potential natural disasters, we can take steps to be prepared to navigate such events. If we live along a fault line, in tornado alley, in a flood zone, or at the base of a volcano, we take precautions: we have a plan of action and an updated stock of supplies. Having these things in order isn't about living in fear of "if" a natural disaster will take place; it is about living as a conscious, cooperative component with nature and moving into action "when" a natural phenomenon happens.

Natural phenomena take place. It's the natural order of things. We can work with them, or we can work against them. We're going to experience these phenomena, there's no way around them, and we do not control them—hard as we may try. The only way for us is *through* the experience. The better prepared we are, the more effectively and efficiently we navigate the process. In this, earthquakes and retrogrades are also similar. We can't control them; however, we can choose to what degree we are controlled by them.

CHAPTER EIGHT ACTION POINTS

Twenty-Two, Twenty-Three, and Twenty-Four

22) DROP, COVER, AND HOLD. Basic earthquake survival training includes an understanding and implementation of the Drop, Cover, and Hold technique: (1) Drop to the floor, (2) get under Cover of a solid surface or up against a weight-bearing wall, and (3) Hold your hands over your head and stay where you are. During a retrograde, a similar practice can be implemented: (1) Drop the need to control, (2) Cover yourself in a bubble wrap of Love, and (3) put a Hold on making any major decisions.

In the midst of a retrograde experience is not the time to create anything new. This is the time to take stock of what we have and where we are and to count our blessings. This process will distract us from relating to the drama of the moment as the truth of what is possible beyond the moment.

23) SHOW UP, SUIT UP, AND SHUT UP. During retrograde or anytime we feel unbalanced, uneasy, and vulnerable, it is important for us to get focused, get clear, and listen. This is not the time to attempt to make sense of the chaos—that will only expand the experience of chaos. This is not the time to be scattered in thoughts, words, and actions that will only create frustration from unfulfillable intentions.

Our focus, like a disco ball reflecting light in all directions, would be better served to be more like a laser beam: focused in one direction and aimed at one subject. As silly as it may sound, retrograde is a great time to work on that coloring book for grown-ups that we purchased on an intuitive hunch.

During chaotic and stressful times, we may feel like pulling out our "invisibility cloaks" and getting off the grid. Yet if we check out, we miss the opportunity to consciously and intentionally be present to what this experience is showing us, the seeing of which will change everything. Suiting up isn't about checking out of the experience but rather about checking into what the experience is providing. To do this, we need to avoid getting caught up in the chaos-as-truth and be willing to ride out the storm with the intention to arrive intact to the clear skies on the other side. This is where suiting up in our protective gear and wrapping ourselves in things that make us feel safe, cozy, and protected—wearing natural fabrics, listening to soothing music, eating organic foods, drinking an abundance of filtered water, etc.—will serve us well in feeling connected and protected.

24) DO WHAT EVERY GOOD GIRL SCOUT AND BOY SCOUT WOULD DO.
Be prepared. Have a Retrograde Survival Kit well-thought-out and appropriately stocked. If we know that meditation and

prayer help us stay connected and grounded, set the intention to do either, or both, more frequently and consistently during the retrograde. If we know that watching funny movies keeps our spirits light, we can have a list of movies at the ready. If we believe in the power of chocolate, we can stock up on a box of sixty assorted Godiva truffles with a ratio favoring dark chocolate raspberry (just sayin'). The point is: do what works for you.

One distinction between a retrograde and earthquakes, tornados, and tsunamis is that retrogrades are trackable. For centuries, astrologers and scientists have been following and projecting the rotation patterns of our solar system with impressive accuracy. All we need is a current Farmer's Almanac, and we can make note of the retrograde schedule in our calendar.

Like any other cycle experience, if we know what we need to support us for the duration of the experience, we can have these supplies at the ready. When we make it a priority to be familiar with what we need to feel grounded and supported during a retrograde, we find ourselves going into the experience with a sense of focus, clarity, and grounding. This preparedness can make all the difference in how we not only navigate the duration of the retrograde but also how we benefit from the experience once we have reached the clearing on the other side. We will feel less unbalanced, less uneasy, and less vulnerable. And, there will be far fewer mental, emotional, and physical messes to clean up.

CHAPTER NINE

COUTURE ESPRIT

Dress Your Spirit

-STRAIGHT TALK-

DRESSING TO EXPRESS YOUR SPIRIT IS a way of announcing to the world that you know who you are. It doesn't cost a million dollars to look like a million bucks. You could walk into a room wearing a gunny sack and, with your spirit-light on high, could be the best-dressed person at the ball. On the other hand, even the highest-end couture can't compensate for a depleted Spirit. If the contents don't match the wrapping ... well, it's like I always say, "You can sprinkle powdered sugar over a pile of poo and call it dessert, but it's still a pile of poo."

- TALK STORY -

Diversity is what makes life an interesting, rich, and full-spectrum experience. If we all look alike, think alike, and act alike, the fashion industry would die, online retailers would crumble, and finding our car in the parking lot of the Mall of America would be a total nightmare. Like black-and-white photography, we need contrast to ignite imagination, fuel expression, and jump-start curiosity.

I am reminded of the story about the white canvas on display in an art exhibit and the artist explaining his vision to a curious observer. When asked by the observer, "What am I looking at?" the artist explains, "A cow eating grass." "Where is the grass?" the observer inquires. "The cow ate it all," the artist proclaims. "Where is the cow?" the observer protests. "Off looking for more grass," the artist insists.

The experience of art is relative. The purpose of art is not to dictate an experience but rather to inspire an experience, to provide the opportunity for an experience to be had. In getting a reaction, in triggering a response, the blank canvas and the canvas exploding with color and light both do their job.

Like the canvas on which the artist is inspired to express himself or herself, people are canvases on which the Soul is inspired to express its Self. Just as an infinite number of Souls express themselves into the world, there are an infinite number of "people canvases" onto and through which these expressions are projected. I like to think of the world as an art gallery and everyone on the planet an original work of art, a unique Soul expression.

I love exploring museums, navigating different genres, and being delighted when I encounter a piece of art that speaks to me in ways unique to a particular moment, in a particular time: when the Spirit of the art awakens the Spirit of the artist within me. Likewise, I love people-watching, each person individually stunning in their expression, making a unique contribution of color and texture to the collective portrait: an organic assembly, aligned for a moment in time, then moving on to the next expression of the human experience.

I was reminded of this when I came across a photo of a woman I had encountered while on vacation in Paris. Paris itself is a work of art—its museums housing an endless collection of any artist or genre one could desire to explore—and the people of Paris are a parade of Soul art in motion.

With an infinite number of opportunities for magical experiences, my travel mates and I decided to walk around a bit and explore while filling time before a winery tour and tasting. The skies were clear and the sun was out in full regalia, and, because of this, the temperature had been toasty for much of the day. We soon abandoned our desire for exploring and replaced it with a search for much-needed shade and a cold beverage. Fortunately, in Paris, with a cafe on most every corner, we were confident such a spot would not be too difficult a goal to achieve.

Within a few minutes, we came upon a cafe patio with a little two-top tucked in a corner beneath a small awning and nestled between the entrance and a potted tree. From this spot, we would be able to sit down, cool off, and people-watch. But first, we would have to make our way through the clusters of tourists and locals huddled around the scattered tables for a midday meal.

Having previously worked as a stage manager at a theme park, I am skilled at navigating large groups of people. Using my six-sensory superpowers, I located the tiniest opening of a path to our table. From experience, I had come to learn how timing is everything. We had to move quickly before our portal of opportunity closed and we were cut off from access to precious drink and shade.

To avoid knocking out any patrons, I hiked up my satchel and, with the grace and speed of a cheetah, sprang into action. Much like Indiana Jones in the opening scene of *Raiders of the Lost Ark*, I launched into navigating our obstacle course.

As I came around the bend, my focus shifted to the image of a single figure seated at a table. A vision of purple perfection, she took my breath away. I had never seen anything like her ... well, in a non-theatre setting anyway. Everything seemed to move in slow motion as I passed her table, my eyes taking in every detail of her magnificence, and I slid into home-base to claim our table. Settling into our corner, I found I was seated with my back to her. I didn't want to be obvious about looking over my shoulder to get another glance, so I took a little more time than I really needed to get adjusted.

There she was—right out of a Toulouse-Lautrec painting—seated by herself, with a lone cappuccino positioned directly in front of her. Her right arm resting on the table beneath her ample bosom, her perfect chin perched atop her left hand as it extended upward from her gracefully anchored elbow. Her doe eyes glancing down and then out onto the passing crowd, with the elegance of a master. And from head to toe, she was dressed in varying shades of purple.

I sat up properly in my chair, knowing any further staring on my part would not only be inappropriate but border on creepy. But I wanted more. I wanted to look at her hard enough to remember her forever, absorbing every detail so I would never forget this vision. But I could not get satiated; I needed more. Something about this woman was calling me to pursue an audience with her.

After placing our beverage order, I took the opportunity to make my move. Confident in my good intentions, I stood up from our table and made my way over to her. I noted how no one seated around her was aware of her presence, as if she had an energetic bubble around her table, rendering her invisible. Even the steady flow of passersby seemed as if not to register her presence. I mean, how could you miss her? She was so out of place and yet Divinely in place. In that moment, I was reminded of a line from a favorite movie, appropriate for this moment, which alludes to how God gets pissed off when we walk past the color purple and don't even notice it.

The expressions on the faces of people walking by who did, in fact, take note were a variety of disbelief, curiosity, and awkward attempts not to stare. It was all I could do to keep from laughing out loud as I witnessed one particular female tourist lock into a projection of judgment as she tried and failed to find a place in her reality for this image of purple eccentricity. Understanding how we, as people, relate to that which is closest to our current reality, it made sense how this tourist with her American costume of (hair) scrunchie, fanny pack (meaning something completely different in Europe), severe panty-lined "yoga" pants, and sneakers could be put off by what she might have perceived to be her Parisian nemesis.

Drawn to the song of my purple siren, I crossed to her table and found myself standing respectfully at the border of the energy bubble surrounding her. She raised her eyes slowly to meet mine. It was clear that an audience with her was something to be earned—not assumed. And since I had not assumed myself into her world, she gave me the nonverbal blink of her diva-endorsed, glamour-length eyelashes, confirming I had been vibrationally vetted and energetically cleared to enter her realm.

Not knowing if she spoke English, and even if she did, what words could be used to express my appreciation for her artistry, I took a breath and, leaning in, said, "I have to say that you are most beautiful."

Her eyebrows rising ever so slightly, the corners of her mouth cupping to form an appreciative smile, she assured me I had offered the appropriate praise. I sensed how, over the years, she had heard these words thousands of times from hundreds of hopeful suiters. I couldn't begin to guess her age, nor would I have even hinted at an attempt to guess. For all I knew, she could have been the star attraction at Moulin Rouge … on opening day. She was timeless, eternal, classic, couture.

With the essence of the Divine Feminine, the eyes of a Sage, and the sultry voice of a Muse, she invited the conversation to continue by asking, "What is your name?"

"My name is Peter."

Reaching out with her free hand, she replied, "I am Vivé."

Taking her hand, I could feel the history of the city in her palm. "It is so nice to meet you."

She asked if this was my first time in Paris and, having informed her that indeed it was, she offered her wishes for a glorious adventure.

I inquired if I could take her photo. Tilting her head to reveal her preferred angle, looking directly into my eyes, she announced, "But of course."

Holding up my cell phone to adjust the framing, Vivé noticed the color of my cell phone case and said, "You like purple too." Pulling my phone to the side of my face, revealing a spirited smile, I confirmed her insight. "Oh, yes. Purple is my favorite color." If I had not already been received into the foyer of her world, my fondness for the color purple would have clinched the deal.

Looking through the camera lens and aligning the frame for the perfect shot, I saw that Vivé appeared isolated from the rest of the world. Every detail of her Soul costume came into focus, from the crown of white curls cascading like a fountain from her head to the regal necklace of stones and lace draping above her bosom. From the flowing tailcoat with its beads and sparkles, along her bangle-drenched wrists, down the form-fitting leggings to their disappearance into a pair of knee-high suede boots, Vivé had dressed her Spirit in purple couture.

I couldn't help but be curious about her story. Her all-knowing expression and the deep well of the mystery in her eyes suggested not only a lifetime of intimate personal encounters but lifetimes of public adventures. What I wouldn't give to sit for hours listening to her share the details of what I could only imagine was an epic tale of life in the City of Light. What lovers had she taken? What shadows in the night had she navigated? What had she seen? What did she know?

I moved quickly to establish my shot, not wanting to overstay my welcome, and with two clicks of the camera had harvested the documentation of our Spirit encounter. I thanked her for her time and generosity, saying, "It was a pleasure to meet you." She offered her hand a final time and assured me the pleasure was mutual. We shared an inner smile, and with my hands placed over my heart, I backed away from her throne, her temple, her sacred space.

Returning to our table, I could not remember my feet contacting the cobblestone patio. Something magical had happened, and I was in need of grounding. I had not only seen a work of art that had called forth an experience of that time and place I would carry with me forever but also had encountered a human canvas, an expression of Spirit, which had called forth the Soul artist within me.

A few sips of my beverage and a moment to get settled into my body, and I was back to the "real world." I sat quietly with my table mates for thirty minutes or so, then, checking the time, we paid our bill, gathered ourselves, got up from our table, and started to make our way to our wine tour reservation. Passing her table on our way out, I stopped for a final offer of appreciation and to bid my purple empress adieu.

With my heart full of appreciation, I offered a Soulfilled, "Au revoir, Vivé. Merci, merci beaucoup." And with a smile to rival the Mona Lisa, Vivé, in her magical way, bid me, "Au revoir, Peter. Au revoir."

As much as I would have loved to have known more about her life, like the master artists, she knew to give me only enough to engage my curiosity, ignite my imagination, and call forth my inner Soul artist to express itself by adding to the canvas the details of my experience. I no longer worried about not having looked "hard enough" to remember all the details of my encounter, for I was confident I would carry the essence of my purple muse with me always.

With a Soulful sense of wonder, we set off for our next adventure. "I just met the Spirit of Paris."

Taking a deep breath and picking up our pace, I was now ready for some great French wine. And with each glass, we would raise a toast, "Vivé la France."

CHAPTER NINE ACTION POINTS

Twenty-Five, Twenty-Six, and Twenty-Seven

25) DON'T JUDGE A BOOK BY ITS COVER. IT JUST MIGHT BE THE BEST BOOK YOU'LL EVER READ. (This is an expanded version of earlier action points intended to support changing our perspective.) Consider that, though our eyes reveal to us what we are seeing, it is our heart that informs what we see. If we are looking at the world through the mind filters of our past, we are only seeing a fraction of what we are looking at. We are only seeing the parts of what we are looking upon that match what our mind filters will allow us to identify as real, facts, and truth. If we allow ourselves to see with our Spirit eyes, with our heart, we will get a more accurate read on the subject while, at the same time, expanding our vision and how we see and experience things beyond the borders of our filters. How often have we judged something as "what is," only to find how mistaken we were when we changed our mood, emotion, or perspective. In other words, when we changed our mind. There was a time when the masses not only thought but *believed* the Earth was flat. We know now that is not the case. Not because the Earth changed its shape but because we've changed our perspective (which changed what we thought were the facts, which changed our truth about the Earth). When our beliefs about the Earth changed from flat to round, our whole world opened up beyond anything we previously imagined possible.

26) BE WILLING NOT TO FIT IN. This behavior can be tricky if we need to be validated by others. Throughout history, many seers have been criticized, ridiculed, and martyred because they spoke openly about what they were able to see that the masses could not. When we see through Spirit eyes and trust what our heart shows us, fitting in can be an intense experience. When we have the confidence to trust what we see, we release any need to fit in, and we no longer seek validation from others. Not to suggest that we give the masses the "bird" but rather to be so self-sufficient that we don't care, give power to, or limit our potential because of what anybody thinks. This isn't about isolating ourselves from the rest of the world; this is about establishing a balance between navigating the world of the "spiritually vision-impaired" and the "clear-seeing through Spirit eyes." It's not one or the other; it's a mastery of both. The ego may fear the experience of standing alone in the crowd, yet when we look at the world through Spirit eyes, we feel more connected to everyone and everything than we ever did when we were trying to fit in.

27) DRESS YOUR SPIRIT. Fashion is all about making a statement. Whether we do it consciously or unconsciously, how we dress is an announcement to the world about how we think (or don't think) about ourselves. Now, this isn't about dressing yourself to prove to the world who you are pretending to be, or trying to convince people who you are, or proving a point. We've all had the experience of seeing someone enter a room "dressed to the nines" and looking like a million bucks on the outside, but something about their vibe just didn't match. You couldn't put your finger on it, but something was wrong. Remember, you can sprinkle powdered sugar on a pile of poo and call it dessert, but it still stinks. And then there are people who walk into a crowded room, their authentic Spirit intact, inner light shining brightly—they could be wearing a burlap sack and still look like a million bucks.

Looking like a million bucks doesn't have to cost a million bucks. This is about accessorizing your Spirit, not maxing your credit card. Whether you're wearing a simple piece of jewelry, a colorful silk scarf, a funky pair of thrift-store shoes, a whimsical hand-painted necktie, or an imported sporty wristwatch, never leave the house without first checking in the mirror to see that you are wearing your Spirit right-side-out. The key is to dress authentic to *your* Spirit. Love is in the details.

PART FOUR
MASTERING OUR HUMANITY

CHAPTER TEN

WHAT ABOUT MY NO AREN'T YOU GETTING?

And, How May I Help You with That?

-STRAIGHT TALK-

UNTIL WE MASTER OUR USE OF the powerful No! we cannot and will not call forth its counterpart, the authentic Yes! Working together, they are power tools for creating and sustaining the integrity of our individual and collective humanity through more effective and efficient communication. The unbalanced energy of a disempowered No and an inauthentic Yes generates chaos and confuses everyone. The clean and straightforward vibration of the powerful No and the authentic Yes are key to establishing the foundation of internal confidence from which we engage the trust and clear-listening of the people we are enrolling as co-creators of our Atonement and the reclaiming of our humanity.

-TALK STORY-

For many, if not most, of us, we were raised to believe it was rude to say No to people when they asked us to do something, even if it was something we didn't want to do or, worse, something we suspected was not in our best interest. As children, we learned mixed messages from this training; it was confusing and set us up to establish an unstable and inconsistent set of values.

As we grow older and find ourselves navigating the "real" world of adulthood in the workforce, dating, marriage, extended family, and as the primary caretaker of children (and the elderly), we find, much of the time, that our mental, emotional, physical, and spiritual investments do not produce the desired results. We are constantly jeopardizing our health and wellness by being agreeable rather than authentic and honest.

WHAT MAKES A NO POWERFUL?

A powerful No comes from a place of clarity grounded in an abiding respect and Love of ourself and, by proxy, everyone. Established in a set of personal boundaries and an unshakeable commitment to our individual and collective health and wellness, the powerful No is confident, unapologetic, and clean. When we take a stand in the energy of our powerful No, no one is confused, especially and foremost ourself.

The powerful No responds rather than reacts. The boundaries established, implemented, and sustained by the powerful No do not protect us from external influences, but rather, they keep our Soul awareness and Source connection unfiltered and uncluttered.

Our powerful No is followed by a period (.) rather than by a comma (,), indicating a statement of completion rather than connecting it to a story of justification and apology. By no means is this meant to shut us down from considering other possibilities or cut us off from the other person. We're just clear on where we stand in response to what has been asked of us and what we are willing to do. If, however, someone inquires about the "Why" of your No, then by all means, enlighten them with facts of your reasoning. This insight, having been invited rather than imposed, could lead the conversation to a reframing of the request. This reframing could shift what has been requested of you into alignment with your availability to offer an authentic Yes.

WHAT CONSTITUTES AN AUTHENTIC YES?

An authentic Yes, like the powerful No, comes from a place of clarity grounded in an established set of personal boundaries, an unshakeable commitment to our individual and collective health and wellness, and an abiding respect and Love of ourself and, by proxy, everyone. The authentic Yes is confident, unapologetic, and clean. When we take a stand in the energy of our authentic Yes, no one is confused, especially and foremost ourself.

The authentic Yes is offered free of the obligation that often evolves into resentment. Again, similar to the powerful No, the authentic Yes is accompanied by a period (.) of completion rather than by a comma (,), connecting it to a story of hesitation and resignation. The boundaries established, implemented, and sustained by the authentic Yes do not bend and bow to the will of the vulnerable fixer, pleaser, or caretaker to gain approval, acceptance, and value. But rather, they are solid in their invulnerable stance, beholden to only that which serves in purpose for the benefit of all concerned. These boundaries are in place not so much to protect us from external influences as to keep our internal sacred inner circle of Soul awareness and Source connection unfiltered and uncluttered.

Having established a practice and pattern of saying Yes when it would have served us better to say No, and having said No when it would have served us better to have said Yes, it can be a tricky task to course-correct ourselves into alignment with a more honest and healthy experience of our authentic Self.

Two key components can make the shift to our powerful No and the authentic Yes an intense workout, both of which can keep us tethered to the training of our people-pleasing dance. First, there is the issue of having trained everyone in our life to expect us to say Yes, while keeping our No to ourselves. We believe that if we were to start saying No, we would hurt the feelings of the people we love (or the people we don't necessarily love, but whom we believe control and influence the surviving and thriving aspects of our life). If we were to suddenly start saying No, we believe we would disappoint people, worrying they will leave us, and we would be destined to find ourselves alone with only the sound of our "No!" bouncing off the walls to keep us company.

Second, for those of us who tend to say Yes when we should say No, there is the issue of FOMO, the Fear of Missing Out. It's a deep-seated concern that if we don't say Yes, we will miss out on a once-in-a-life opportunity. So we say, Yes to everything, *everything*!

The amount of time, energy, and effort invested in the circus act of keeping all of our Yes and No plates spinning is exhausting, jeopardizing our mental, emotional, physical, and spiritual health. Having surrendered control of our free will to external influences, we find ourselves drained of our internal life-force. From this place of feeling depleted, we find ourselves using Yes and No as survival tools—anything to get through the day "alive."

However, the powerful No and the authentic Yes are not survival tools or, worse, in their darkest and most toxic form, assault weapons of manipulation. Rather, they are power tools for setting and managing our boundaries for health, wellness, abundance, happiness, joy, and fulfillment. When we use our Yes and our No with integrity and mastery, we are showing up in the world as powerhouse creators of our world, modeling confidence and clarity, and serving as examples of living an authentic, thriving life.

Once we have accomplished managing ourselves in navigating the powerful No and the authentic Yes in reference to the external influences in our life, it is next appropriate for us to shift the same intention and practice to managing our powerful No and authentic Yes internally. It is all well and good to become efficient and effective in navigating how we engage with other people with clarity and integrity. However, to master the power of our No and the authenticity of our Yes, we must fuel them with the integrity of our internal Soul awareness and launch them from our internal Source connection.

It is important here to consider why, at this point, we are focusing on developing our relationship with the powerful No and the authentic Yes with external influences first. If our At-One-Ment and reclaiming our humanity is an inside job, one might think it more appropriate and effective to begin working these power tools internally and move outward from there. That makes sense. However, working the tools with external influences first is more efficient and effective in supporting our sustainable mastery of the tools.

In my experience of my mind filter retraining and having facilitated hundreds of people through their personal process, I have found it can be overwhelming, discouraging, and counterproductive to enter internal combat with the Goliath-hold our egos have on our beliefs. When we move inside for the internal mastering of our powerful No and our authentic Yes, there is no timeout and no walking away from the encounter. The internal work of mastering our At-One-Ment and reclaiming our humanity is a twenty-four-seven gig. It is the most confronting work we will ever do because we cannot walk away from it. Wherever we go, there we are.

Developing our skill set while practicing on external influences first allows us to take breaks between rounds. We can say No to (fill in the blank), then walk away, go home, have a glass of wine, process the experience, and rest up before going back onto the court for another round.

If the internal journey were easy, everyone would be doing it. It takes courage, faith, commitment, and a willingness to stand emotionally, mentally, physically, and spiritually "naked" before the mirror of our beliefs, calling ourselves out and up from the deep sleep of illusion-as-truth in which we have been living. Once awake, we can pivot our focus onto our reflection in the unfiltered mirror of our potential. It is here we begin to acclimate to our At-One-Ment, and from here, we are positioned to claim and sustain our humanity in its highest potential.

So, let's be clear to keep the horse before the cart, so to speak, and work our tools at the appropriate pace and in the appropriate place to support our mastery of the powerful No and the authentic Yes.

Becoming conscious of the conversation we are having in our mind between our human intellect and our Soul wisdom is where we iron out the wrinkles of the data that inform how we use our No and our Yes. Working through the mind filters of our life experience, we are attempting to fit our potential into the box of what "we already know we know" about life and how the world works. In this, we are using only a fraction of the infinite knowledge we have access to as extensions and expressions of infinite Source. From this place of limited thinking, we can only say No and Yes to what we recognize as familiar, based on what we have already established within the parameter of what we believe is our achievable potential.

The work of the ego is to keep us safe, and yet, not having ever been given a job description with a set of constructive guidelines as a reference for thriving, the ego has had to rely on its own sense of survival to keep us alive. It identifies anything unfamiliar as a threat and will use any means to distract us from venturing into the unknown. The most effective of its tools is the broadcasting of the data of our past, filed in the mind filters of our mental and emotional life training. Remember the elephant and the string?

It doesn't usually take much for the ego to keep us in line, as we are well-trained in saying Yes to the familiar of what "we already know we know" and No to the unfamiliar of what "we don't know we don't know." However, should we get too curious about exploring the unknown and begin to lean in the direction of trying something different, something new, the ego will not hesitate to pull out all the stops and use its fully loaded assault weapon ... the voice of your mother. Or, to be fair, any authority figure whose voice we have been trained to offer our surrender. It is to these internal voices, to our mind filter training, and to our resistance to our individual potential that we must master the use of our powerful No and the authentic Yes.

When we move these mind filters of limiting beliefs to the side, a process I call the Mind Filter Combover, we create unobstructed access to the clear guidance of our internal Source connection. In this clearing, the powerful No and the authentic Yes are revealed to us in their purest form.

Managing our human experience from our Source awareness perspective is the most profound footing from which to establish the mastery of our internal powerful No and our authentic Yes. Anchored in the expansive Love that is our Soul connection in pure positive Source energy, we are better able to navigate external influences with profound clarity and the strength of grace. From this place of integrity, we can be confident our powerful No and our authentic Yes are in the best interests of our individual health and wellness, for the benefit of all concerned, and grounded in the At-One-Ment of our humanity.

Who knew so much behind-the-scenes work is invested in our every No and Yes? It can be overwhelming when you think about it. How on earth do we get to the place of habitual mastery of the powerful No and the authentic Yes? It's like the joke about the musician wandering the streets of New York City, carrying a violin case, asking a local for directions. "How do I get to Carnegie Hall?" to which the local replies, "Practice, practice, practice." With practice, we will come to master each powerful No and authentic Yes with clarity, respect, and Love of ourself and, by proxy, everyone.

CHAPTER TEN ACTION POINTS

Twenty-Eight, Twenty-Nine, and Thirty

28) WHEN YOU SAY NO, MEAN IT. By itself, your No has no power. Like all words, it is a symbol. It is the energy and clarity behind the No that breathes life into it and gives it power. If your No is uncertain, hesitant, apologetic, manipulative, controlling, resistant, or not-worthy, not only will you confuse others, but you, yourself, will be confused by the less-than-desirable results you are manifesting.

29) WHEN YOU HEAR NO, GET IT. Honoring someone's No can be a powerful and empowering experience. When we accept and honor someone's No, the person feels heard and respected. This can change the person's listening of you and give them the opportunity to put your request through their own vetting process, reconsider it, and, if appropriate, create the space for the question/request/invitation to be resubmitted. To be clear, this isn't manipulating someone's No into a Yes—it's about releasing your attachment to their No and creating the space for something else. The key is to honor the person's No, complete the interaction, and move on. Remember, honoring one person's powerful No can redirect your focus and create a clearing, which leads you to a (more appropriate) authentic Yes.

30) PRACTICE THE CONSCIOUS AND INTENTIONAL YES. Vetting your Yes can be one of the most profound and effective ways of showing up in your life. When your Yes is grounded in "for-the-benefit-of-all-concerned" and fueled with the life-force of Love, the entire Universe is queued up to support you with everything you need to navigate a fully-realized experience and manifest expansive results—beyond what you know to be possible. Give it a try and be willing to be inspired.

CHAPTER ELEVEN

WHEN WE CHANGE OUR MIND, WE CAN CHANGE OUR WORLD

-STRAIGHT TALK-

WITH ADVANCEMENTS IN TECHNOLOGY, SCIENCE, AND MEDICINE, we are sitting on a gold mine of human potential unlike anything we have ever seen before. With the sacred institutions of religion and government, we can create and establish the foundation on which to launch and sustain the next expression of our evolved human potential. With this profound potential comes profound responsibility; with this sacred structure comes sacred accountability. The measure of both is determined by the integrity of our humanity.

−TALK STORY−

The state of our humanity informs our experience of the world rather than our world informing our humanity. With our humanity intact, we create thriving advances in our human experience, the likes of which we could only have previously imagined. Without our humanity intact, we generate a self-imposed survival of our human experience, the likes of which we would not have dared to imagine. We use the same tools to create both experiences. However, the tools themselves only construct the symbols of our potential. It is the state of mind and intention behind the use of these tools that inform thriving or surviving results.

When the integrity of our humanity is jeopardized, we become a culture of unconscious (willing) participants surrendering logic, intuition, and our humanity over to what we perceive to be the most convenient and accessible answers, modalities, influences, and leaders. With advances in technology, science, and medicine, we have access to profound tools to nurture, expand, and evolve our human experience. With the internet, we are more connected than ever before, yet we feel more isolated and alone than ever before. With science, we have access to a limitless understanding of the workings of the Universe, yet we have a chronic discomfort with the inner workings of our own minds. With medicine, we are living longer than humans have ever lived, yet we are more diseased with a wider range of illnesses than any previous generation. Why is this?

Currently, we find ourselves, as we have so many times before, at a defining moment on the spectrum of our evolution. Like every generation before us, it is our turn to contribute to the progression of the human race, taking what we inherited from our ancestors, expanding on it, and nurturing it in preparation for handing it off to the next generation. We are stewards of this great experiment, an eternal work in progress; we never get it done, and we cannot get it wrong. However, exercising our free will, we can choose (and, make no mistake about it, we do choose) to make progress with either the strength of conscious and intentional thriving grace or the deficiency of surviving naivety.

Reminiscent of the first segment in Disney's animated classic *Fantasia, the Sorcerer's Apprentice*, we have found ourselves with access to powerful creative tools. In the fantastical setting of this story, Mickey Mouse, as the title character, one day finds himself seduced by the magical powers of his master's wand and chooses to give it a test drive, all while the Sorcerer is out of the castle running errands. Armed with an abundance of curiosity, a childlike wonder, and insufficient knowledge, he picks up the wand. With a few waves in the air, all hell breaks loose as the Sorcerer's power tool becomes, in the hand of the innocent Mickey Mouse, the apprentice's assault weapon. The wand itself didn't change; it was the mind informing the hand operating the wand that made the difference between creating harmony, order, and beauty—OR—manifesting overwhelming chaos in the form of (among other things) a parade of pink elephants and a tutu-toting hippo.

With the invention of the World Wide Web, we can communicate globally at lightning speed, providing the opportunity to share ideas, emotions, and beliefs with the push of a button. Social media has the capacity to bring us together and unite us unlike any other time in the history of the human race. Yet, without intellectual development, emotional maturity, and social discipline, we have (in a relatively short period of time) managed to unleash a tsunami of unconscious rantings and, at times, a conscious and intentional toxic agenda of mind manipulation.

This is not to say there isn't an abundance of goodwill and celebration of humanity circulating the globe through social media. An abundance of goodwill far exceeds the alternative. However, as humans, we find what we're looking for, in that we attract and relate to that which is the closest match to our chronic vibrational/thought offering. Thus, when we are individually and collectively fatigued, our mental, emotional, physical, and spiritual health is compromised, making us the victims, as well as the perpetrators, of toxic postings. The internet is just the internet; it doesn't decide what is good, bad, right, or wrong. It just *is*. It is, however, the mindset of the user of the internet that must be held accountable for how it is navigated.

Being indifferent, the internet can be a power tool for humanity or an inhumane assault weapon. We get to choose.

With the profound advancements of science, we have an amazing tool to assist us in articulating an understanding of the inner workings of the Universe. However, it is when we step out of integrity with science as a power tool that we raise it up to Golden Calf status and use it in the name of righteousness. Without humility and humanity, science can become an assault weapon. Take, for example, the atomic bomb. The scientist who figured out how to split the atom did so out of curiosity. It was never a conscious intention to use the discovery for inhumane purposes.

In our humility and our humanity, we never lose sight of the fact that the contribution of science is to discover, articulate, and expand on what has already been created. There is a joke about a scientist having a conversation with God (which is kind of funny in and of itself), claiming how he could create a man, just as God had created man. God enthusiastically, in His all-knowing and all-loving way, gave His blessing and encouraged the scientist to have a go at it. As the scientist reached, with cupped hands, to the ground, God inquired as to what he was doing. When the scientist explained he was picking up dirt, the key ingredient in the recipe for making man, God laughed. "Nice try. Make your own dirt."

Through research, discovery, and the assembling of facts, science has developed a language for helping us wrap our minds around the great mysteries of our tangible world and the infinite Universe. Science, however, by its own design, is not the Truth. For the Truth, being Truth, does not require defining to be true. If science were the Truth, it would not redefine itself every ten years or so with each series of advancements. Inspired by curiosity, the beauty of science is its hunger for understanding, its commitment to exploring the unknown, and its ability to master the articulation of the findings. And in doing so, it provides us the opportunity to feel more connected and validated with our part in the big picture. At its essence, science is man's attempt to understand and articulate the ineffable. Science, then, is a work in progress: an always-evolving process with infinite potential. Our humility and our humanity are key components in the advancements of science as a power tool.

When it comes to the profound lifesaving developments in medicine, we have, at times, wandered far from the path of our humanity and fallen under the influence of the business of pill-pushing, generating the clientele necessary to keep a multi-billion-dollar industry thriving. And, to sustain the industry, a pill-popping mindset must be created and then convinced it must have the product at all costs to stay alive. (To be fair, in order for a culture to be seduced by a manipulative influence, the culture must first believe it is diseased and powerless to save itself.) Add to this an unregulated insurance industry and a steady stream of newly discovered diseases, and we have the ideal model for supply and demand.

This is not to say the advances in medicine aren't spectacular and even miraculous. But what we have forgotten to bring into the equation is how the authentic healing of any disease, be it emotional, mental, physical, or spiritual, is influenced by the mindset of the patient.

A distinction in *A Course In Miracles* instructs the teacher and the student alike to use the tools of this world but do not be deceived by them. In other words, the awesome advances in medicine are tools to be used to support the patient in the patient's healing process. For medicine to be effective in its healing potential, the patient must reclaim the healing power of their own mind and become a cooperative component in their individual healing process.

Many Western doctors are beginning to implement this approach into their interactions with both patients and support staff, embracing and integrating the teachings of thousands of years of Eastern medicine. The effectiveness and sustainability of the shift in this awareness ride on honoring the presence of our humanity. When patients and practitioners come to the healing process with the power of their humanity intact, rather than with quotas they are pressured to meet and prescriptions they are forced to fill, then medicine can be navigated as the power tool it is designed to be in support of the healing process.

To make the shift from unconscious naivety to conscious intention, it is imperative that we consider what we are working with—the tools we are using to create our reality and manifest our highest potential. As is the case with any tool, it is important to understand its purpose and potential, how to use it safely and effectively, and to be clear on what we intend to achieve. Much like a chef's knife, picked up by the handle, it is an artisan's tool; picked up by the blade, it becomes a self-inflicting assault weapon. Social media, science, and medicine are profound tools with expansive potential. Like any tool, they can be a power tool for thriving or an assault weapon of self-destruction, depending on how we use them, the power we give them, and the intention with which we use them. Our reclaimed and nurtured humanity is the foundation on which we launch the effectiveness of any tool we use to evolve and expand our experience. The choice is ours.

Similar to science, religion is man's attempt to articulate an understanding of creation and the Creator, thus establishing a foundation on which this understanding may be nurtured and a structure established through which the 'flock" can be managed, guided, and protected. In a sense, religion and science are two sides of the same coin.

At the core of each religion is an authentic good intention. However, in far too many cases, good intention has given way to the influence of agendas, many of which are in the name of God yet, over time, have fallen out of alignment with the Will of God. Consider the conversations, debates, and fights (aka wars) over evolution versus creation versus Divine intelligence. What if attempting to define and establish the three as distinct is an impossible task, as impossible as attempting to define the Holy Trinity as three independent entities—the Father separate from the Son, separate from the Holy Spirit? It's not possible to separate what is whole, complete, and Divine. When religion demands that it be separate from, better than, or truer than, it is no longer representative of the Mind of God. When we surrender over our humanity in blind faith to misinformed and misguided influences, we stop listening to our inner Source and cut ourselves off from our natural direct and unfiltered Divine guidance.

Similar to religion, effective politics and efficient governing are man's way of creating and managing a societal structure designed to nurture, support, and sustain the coexistence of the masses. Without some sort of governing structure in place, chaos can take hold of society, yet with too much structure, the life-force can be sucked out of human potential, and the creative muscles atrophy. A conscious and intentional balancing is required to sustain any form of politics and governing. The success of this balancing act relies on the health and wellness of the individual as well as the collective at the emotional, mental, physical, and spiritual levels. Like the cells of the human body, when the members of a society fall out of alignment with the greater good, disease sets in and, if not course-corrected, will manifest a cultural cancer.

Is it possible to claim and sustain a political and governing balance? Absolutely. However, will we claim and sustain a balance? Not likely. It is not likely humanity will ever settle into one form of politics or one style of governing—not because we are not capable, but because too many variables are at play. We are a part of the great experiment, a work in progress. We didn't come here to lock into one way of Being and ride it out for all eternity. We are part of an ever-evolving and expanding eternal process. We will never get it done, and having free will, we will never get it wrong. We can (and will) only navigate it for intervals, fluctuating between the grace of thriving and the struggle of surviving. Because of this, it is key to our health and wellness, in all areas, to be cooperative components in our individual and collective well-being. Our humanity is our navigation system, our Divine GPS. How we show up with each breath, in alignment with our healthy and balanced humanity, is the only thing we have control over and the most profound tool at our disposal.

Books and essays by the hundreds of thousands have been researched, written, and published on these topics. Lectures and workshops have been mastered and facilitated with the intent to bring clarity and the hope of healing, yet rather than healing, we have created a culture of well-read workshop junkies looking for the next fix. We have surrendered our potential to the hopes of the one-word healing, the magic pill, the guru, or the messiah—the One "out there" who will save us, fix things for us, and make our problems go away. The time has come to Old-Yeller that shit. Our humanity is an *inside* job.

When we become a culture fixated on looking to the symptoms for the answers, we completely dismiss the source of our dis-ease. Our focus on the symptoms generates a demand for supplies to address these symptoms. In this, we have created and sustained multibillion-dollar industries to support and enable us in remaining locked into the symptoms as the truth and denying access to our healing through working with the source of our dis-ease.

Be cautious to not judge this as good, bad, right, wrong, or indifferent. We are identifying the facts of where we have landed and where we find ourselves at this point in our evolution. These facts aren't the truth of our potential; they are just the reality of where we find ourselves in our dis-eased cultural mindset and the "what-is" of where we are. However, they do not in any way dictate our potential—that, we can turn on a dime and course-correct at any time and at any moment. With a shift in consciousness and a fine-tuning of our thoughts, words, and actions, we can change our minds, and as a result, we change our world.

With a change of mind, we can use the internet to nurture and advance our humanity while holding ourselves accountable for managing our use for the benefit of all concerned as our number one priority, responsibility, and desire. With a redefining of purpose, we can reap the profound benefits of science as it continues to support us in understanding the workings of the Universe and our place in the bigger picture. With a shift in consciousness and reclaiming our mind-over-matter potential, we can redirect our medical research to address diseases at their source and develop preventative medicinal options. With a reconnection to our faith as an expression of our Source, we breathe the life of Divine back into our religion. When We the People act for the benefit of all concerned, electing vetted representatives who are a vibrational match for our self-nurtured humanity, we can navigate effective politics and efficient governing through the full spectrum of our evolutionary process. The key to all of this is held in how we manage our individual and, by proxy, our collective humanity. Shift internally, act locally, manifest globally.

CHAPTER ELEVEN ACTION POINTS

Thirty-One, Thirty-Two, Thirty-Three

31) BE AN ONLINE ADVOCATE FOR HUMANITY AT ITS BEST. Social media can be a power tool for humanity **or** an assault weapon for its downfall. We only need a basic understanding of the Law of Attraction to make this connection. It's not rocket science or brain surgery: What we focus on, we attract. To this point, it is our free will to create whatever we choose, and we do, whether consciously or unconsciously. The Universe does not distinguish between good or bad, right or wrong, high or low. The Universe is a Yes machine. Whatever we give our focus to, it says Yes to.

Taking this awareness into consideration, why not be conscious and intentional about what we post into the world of social media? One way to effectively manage ourselves into being cooperative components in the world we create is to have a reliable vetting process in place. Try this: Before posting anything on social media, ask yourself, "Is this something I want to put out into the world to magnify a thousandfold and have come back at me for me to experience?" If the answer is Yes, post it. If the answer is No, delete it. It's that simple.

Our ego will give us grief about this practice, only because the ego is hell-bent on being right about anything and everything. But at what price? When we introduce the consideration of price into the equation, we are more likely to think twice about posting a toxic contribution to the gumbo of social media. This consideration isn't about being a good or pleasant or politically correct person. This is so much more expansive and profound than that. This "healthy pause" is all about being clear on how we want to show up in the world, represent ourselves in our culture, and what we want to attract and create as our experience.

If you are having a particularly bad day and feel inclined to share of your experience on social media, by all means, go for it. However, be clear that by doing so, you will be expanding the experience of your discomfort. If you need to let off steam, at least take ownership of what you are doing. Be accountable for how you are participating, and when the energy of the expanded version of that post comes back at you, take accountability for how you created your experience. Likewise, if you are having a particularly good day, by all means, spread the wealth. Be equally willing to be accountable for generating and receiving the expanded version of your contribution.

Note: Raising the consciousness and vibration of social media not only sets us up to expand our experience of humanity at its best, and it also makes it difficult for hackers and cyber trolls to go undetected. High-vibrational conscious social media participation is to hackers what garlic and sunlight are to (energy) vampires.

32) UPDATE YOUR INTERNAL WIRING BY DOING MORE OF WHAT YOU LOVE. Begin taking steps to become a cooperative component in your mental, emotional, physical, and spiritual wellness. The best preventative medicine is to do more of what you Love. Most diseases are diagnosed well into the manifestation of the disorder, suggesting that most diseases are unconsciously manifested and become a conscious experience only after being diagnosed. This perspective makes sense, for who in their right mind would consciously create a disease? Doing more of what we Love as a way of life is a more preventative than reactive form of medicine.

The human body is susceptible to falling out of alignment with its wiring for health and wellness. That's a fact. However, because of how the brain is wired and its part in the design of the physical body as a whole, there is a built-in course-corrective component for realignment into its natural state of health and wellness. This powerful component is our mind. Bottom line: when we are in a chronic state of Love, we attract and manifest in-kind. When we are in a chronic state of not-Love, we attract and manifest in-kind. It's that simple … and that complex.

Now, to be responsible, it is important to understand that disease happens, and it is part of the human physical body experience. However, it is possible to de-manifest the range of diseases and the medications required to address these diseases by a considerable amount. Patients are baffling doctors all the time with miraculous recoveries and healing. In almost all of the cases (in ALL of these cases), the patient's shift in consciousness triggers the healing process. The patient changes their mind, the brain sends different signals, and the cells of the body respond. Think of the brain as a computer, the cells as computer programing, and the mind as the computer programmer. In medicine, being a tool of this physical world, a temporary and profound support system is established to aid the healing process. The key to effective medicine is the alignment of the mind with health and wellness.

Some will argue it is not possible to cure a disease just because we change our mind about the disease. And they would be correct. If we create what we give our focus to, whether we want it or not, we have to change our mind about our health and wellness, not the disease, and turn our focus to **only** our health and wellness.

33) PRAY AND VOTE IN ALIGNMENT WITH YOUR HIGHEST GOOD. When we pray in fear, we can only attract and hear answers and guidance that match our fear. This is so, not because our prayers are unworthy of being heard and answered by a punitive and exclusivist God—good heavens no. Our prayers are always answered by an all-Loving and all-Powerful Creator.

We just can't hear the all-Loving and all-Powerful voice of the Creator when we are locked into fear-listening. We are much like transistor radios in that if we are dialed up to KFEAR when we pray, and the answer to our prayers is being broadcast on KFAITH, all we're going to hear is static. To receive the answer to our prayers accurately, we must first change our frequency setting to align with the broadcast (God-cast, if you will) of the higher guidance.

It is understandable how, when we are in the mental and energetic loop of fear, it is not always a clear path to adjusting our alignment. It's part of the human experience to forget and then to remember our birthright of our direct connection to Source. Fortunately, the genius of Source has provided an option by which answers and guidance can reach us through alternate means. Charity, for example, in its purest form, is God's way of gifting to us, through others, that which we believe we are unable to manifest for ourselves. Not because we are unworthy of God's direct guidance but because, in our fear, we cannot hear the guidance that is at our fingertips.

The same can be said for how we cast our vote. We vote for the candidate and issues that are the closest vibrational match for our chronic vibrational mindset. We vote to elect messengers to represent us in the political and governing structure. The personalities we elect to office could then be likened to mirrors of our collective mindset: poster children for the chronic cultural mindset.

Because of this, it is profoundly important that the representatives we attract are vetted to be as free of filters and agendas that run counter to our health, wellness, and humanity as is humanly possible. We become conscious and cautious in our choices because we understand how surrendering our personal power over to unvetted external influence can jeopardize our individual and collective emotional, mental, physical, and spiritual health and wellness. And in this, our humanity is compromised.

This awareness applies to both our religious and political climates. We attract what we focus on, whether we want it or not. If we want "better," we have to do "better" by Being "better." The starting point of this shift in consciousness begins always, and in all ways, with our thoughts, words, and actions—our most profound and influential tools and the only tools we have control over.

It is important to consider there is more good than not-good in the world, by far. More awakened and awakening people are in the world than we know, by far. There are more opportunities for Divine interactions than not, by far. The only difference in our experience of the thriving or surviving version of our humanity is in how we use our minds. Change our minds, and we change our world.

Bottom line: Be conscious and intentional to check in with your emotional and vibrational offering *before* launching your prayer and casting your vote. Aim high for the benefit of all concerned. Understand that like attracts like, and we can raise the vibration of our offering with the confidence that we are cooperative components in manifesting the highest potential of our humanity.

CHAPTER TWELVE

AT-ONE-MENT

The Soul of Our Humanity

—STRAIGHT TALK—

OUR JOURNEY THROUGH *AT-ONE-MENT: RECLAIMING OUR HUMANITY* has reconnected us with the importance, value, and influence of the role our conscious (and unconscious) participation plays in our evolution as a human race. We have reawakened to the awareness of how our experience is always a direct reflection, reaction, and response to how we are showing up and navigating our thoughts, words, and actions. We have been reminded of the gift of our free will and the influence our chronic vibrational offering has in creating what we focus on, whether we want it or not. Understanding how we show up, participate, and promote the nurturing of our human potential is our power tool, putting at our fingertips access to our humanity's infinite possibility.

-TALK STORY-

Key to the success of our efforts is understanding how our humanity is an inside job. We do not change the world by manipulating, controlling, and forcing external influences. This way of Being only distracts us from being effective and diminishes our efforts, leaving us fatigued, depleted, and defeated. We have never created anything we wanted from an unvetted, fear-driven, survival perspective. We have always created what we want when we do so from a conscious and intentional commitment for the benefit of all concerned, always and in all ways, no exceptions.

HUMANITY

1: compassionate, sympathetic, or generous behavior or disposition: the quality or state of being humane

2: the quality or state of being human

Time and again, we have seen how natural or human-generated disasters bring people together in ways unlike what we experience at other times. Under these unimaginable and intense conditions, the human Spirit rises to the foreground, crossing without question any geographic, social, political, racial, and religious boundaries. In these extended moments, our humanity overrides all else, and we are connected in ways that inspire, drive, and empower—magnifying physical strength, emotional and intellectual clarity, and elevating our humanity to its highest potential. In all of these cases, our humanity is not created by the conditions of these events; rather, its presence is magnified in its sustained unfiltered state of purity.

Our humanity is always (and in all ways) present within our individual and collective potential. However, the degree to which it is nurtured, practiced, and mastered is our free will. When we get distracted by the self-imposed workings of the "real" world (and let's be straight about this: they *are* self-imposed), our humanity can get displaced to the back burner of our awareness. Its eternal pilot light ignited and always at a simmer, our humanity is never unavailable for liberation and expression. The key to the mastery of our humanity at its highest potential is to move it to the forefront of our awareness as a conscious and intentional articulation of who we believe ourselves to Be.

Doing this from our human mental, emotional, and physical perspective alone limits our awareness to what we already know about the workings of humans, the world at large, and life in general. Our understanding (and thus our belief) around what is possible is developed through experiences, either our own or inherited. In this, we have left out our most influential, accurate, and empowering perspective and awareness. To be effective in claiming and sustaining the emotional, mental, physical, and spiritual health and wellness of our humanity, we must first manage and navigate our individual emotional, mental, physical, and spiritual alignment with the Truth of who we are at our core: our Soul.

SOUL

1: the immaterial essence, animating principle,
or actuating cause of an individual life

2: the spiritual principle embodied in human beings,
all rational and spiritual beings, of the universe

3: a person's total self

4: the moral and emotional nature of human beings

5: spiritual or moral force

We are invited here to consider the possibility that our humanity is a vehicle on which our Soul expresses itself. When our humanity is in alignment with this awareness, we have a healthy, Soulful experience of ourselves and our world. When our humanity is out of alignment with this awareness, we have a dis-eased, Soulless experience of ourselves and our world. In this, we might say that the state of our humanity is an expression of Soul consciousness.

At an appropriate point in every awakening process, every spiritual journey, every shift in enlightenment, we have the profound experience of facing our Soul status head-on. At some point, we have to suck it up and deal with the Truth of who we are as Souls having a human experience. There is just no way around it. We can deny it (and we do deny it); however, if we are to get serious about being cooperative components in the evolution of our humanity fully-realized to its highest potential, we have to bring our Soul status into the equation. And it is here we must choose to shift, or get off the pot, so that we may start generating results in alignment with what we say we really want to create.

So, what is the Soul, who are we as Soul, and how do we tap into this awareness as a sustainable component in the evolution of our humanity? This expansive topic has as many interpretations as there are people on the planet: previously, currently, and pending. However, it is possible to rally around basic understandings that leave room for the branching off of interpretations without disconnecting from the life-force of our Soul roots.

For the sake of this conversation and the intention of establishing a common ground on which to rally, let us consider how we are all whole, complete, and Divine extensions of Source, expressions of God. The life-force that is Source, God, is the same life-force that animates our human physical bodies. It is the life-force that is projected into our physical body at the beginning of our physical life and retracted from our physical body upon the completion of our physical life experience. This life-force is pure positive Source energy, eternal and Divine by design, always non-physical, and sometimes expressed in the physical.

To further support this conversation, it is advised to position our relationship to God, the idea of God, or any resistance to the concept of God, in as non-dogmatic a perspective as possible. Use whatever name for the Source-of-everything that fills your heart with, and liberates your mind to, Love. This is your most sacred relationship. Keep it clear of mental, emotional, physical, and spiritual obstacles.

Being extensions of Source and expressions of God, we can never not be connected to our Source, to God. In this, we are all connected at our Source, in God. Everyone, all-inclusive, no exceptions, always, and in all ways. As confronting and overwhelming as this concept can be to our human ego and intellect, allow yourself to hear this with your heart rather than your brain. Your heart knows this is True, and it will, with your consent, find a way to work around any perceived obstacles of belief that run counter to this awareness.

When we allow ourselves to consider, even for a moment, our Source/God connection, we see and experience ourselves in the Light of our Truth. From this perspective, we are positioned to see and experience everyone and everything in the Light of this Truth. When we allow ourselves to sustain our perspective in this awareness, we generate thoughts, words, and actions in alignment with our Source connection. In other words, we see and experience ourselves, everyone, and everything Soul to Soul in the frequency of Love.

ATONEMENT

1: the exemplifying of human(ity's) oneness with God

This concept can be confronting for the human intellect and ego to wrap around, to the point of inducing resistance in the form of mild to extreme retaliation. Throughout human history, humans have fought against humans to prove separation is the truth, all the while ignorant to the Truth that separation is impossible. The pain inflicted and experienced in the name of being "right" is induced without considering how, being expressions of the same Source, whatever we do to another, we do to ourselves, and whatever we do to ourselves, we do to the collective. There is no mystery here. It's pretty straightforward when we know what we're working with and do so with an open heart and a clear, intentional mind.

Considering how what we do to ourselves, we do to the collective, we can see how our humanity is an inside job—establishing a conscious relationship with our internal emotional, mental, physical, and spiritual alignment. Our understanding of Self as "Soul having a human experience" and bringing this awareness to our thoughts, words, and actions positions us to be most effective and efficient in our contribution to the evolution of humanity.

AT-ONE-MENT

We as One

To be clear, it is important to understand there is no way on earth, literally, that everyone will be on the same page, frequency, perspective, agenda, or intention for any sustainable amount of time. That is not only unrealistic, but it is also not appropriate given the purpose of the human experience—and its contribution to the evolution of the Soul while navigating Soul Lessons and Soul Agreements. Humanity and the world at large are a work in progress. As stated in previous chapters, this isn't about reaching a goal and riding it out for all eternity. Diversity, contrast, and change are our strengths: they are what make this life and this world interesting. Can you imagine a world filled with stagnant, like-minded people walking around with perpetual blissed-out expressions on their faces? Honestly, how long would that be interesting before we needed to stir things up to feel alive?

Contrast, which fuels creativity, is key to the richness of the human experience. Given that we are creative beings—expressions of our Creator and participating in a creative work in progress—contrast is our creative power tool. When we navigate our human creative process with our Soul awareness perspective intact, we create humanity at its magnificent potential. When we attempt to navigate this same process in the absence of our Soul awareness, creativity becomes an assault weapon manifesting struggle, hardship, despair, and inhumanity. Both paths are valid given our Source birthright of free will. However, we need only dwell in the shadow side of the creative process long enough to identify what we do *not* desire so that we can be inspired to identify what we *do* desire, pivot our focus, and course-correct our efforts in the direction of the Soulful potential of each experience. There is no need to take up residence in the shadow side of any experience beyond its purpose of inspiring us otherwise. We have a choice.

However, whatever we choose, we need to get real about having exercised our free will to choose and get clear about our part in this process, our individual contribution, and hold ourselves accountable for having chosen to participate in alignment (or out of alignment) with the Soul of our humanity at its best.

Of course, at times, our life doesn't look like what we thought it would or should look like; we stand in the middle of a moment where nothing is recognizable as being in alignment with our emotional, mental, physical, and spiritual health and wellness. That is a part of being human. However, during these moments, we have the profound opportunity to pivot our focus away from external influences as the truth of our potential, course-correcting our thoughts, words, and actions into alignment with our internal Soul awareness. In this, we are aware that what we are "doing" is irrelevant to who we are Being while we are "doing" what we are doing. Being that how we show up is the ONLY thing we have control over, taking control over how we are showing up is the most profound way we can effectively and efficiently contribute to the health and wellness of our humanity. We are always appropriately positioned to be of the highest service to humanity. How we show up, however, determines the degree to which we are efficient, effective, and fulfilled.

Managing our thoughts, words, and actions into alignment with our Soul awareness is a moment-by-moment, breath-by-breath practice. An appropriate analogy for staying on course with this is that of an airline captain piloting a plane.

If you are flying an airplane from LA to NYC, it is important to keep the plane flying on course. Left to its own accord and vulnerable to the influence of the weather patterns, the airplane will constantly find itself veering off course, if ever so slightly at first, for the entire journey. Without course-correction, a slightly off-course status can, over time, evolve into a dramatic and traumatic rerouting. Rather than arriving in NYC and making the curtain for your favorite Broadway show, you might end up chewing on the catch-of-the-day at a diner in Newfoundland. Oops.

Navigating our Soul awareness and managing our thoughts, words, and actions, much like the airplane captain, requires our constant conscious intention and attention. Course-correcting our vibrational offering in each moment, with each breath, is key to a sustainable alignment with our At-One-Ment and reclaiming our humanity.

CHAPTER TWELVE ACTION POINTS

Thirty-Four, Thirty-Five, Thirty-Six

34) RE-MEMBER OUR PURPOSE BY REMEMBERING WHO WE ARE.

REMEMBER OUR SOUL PURPOSE: From our Soul perspective, our Purpose is to remember who we are as the whole, complete, and Divine expression of Source, an extension of God. That's it, that's all there is to it, and that is the ALL of it.

REMEMBER OUR HUMAN PURPOSE: From our human, physical world perspective, our Purpose is the projection of our Soul Purpose in the form of our contribution to the evolution of humanity: what we bring to the world to nurture, inspire, and evolve.

When we are in Purpose, we are informed and driven by passion, compassion, and a sense of belonging to something bigger than ourselves. Our Purpose is not something we find, force, or create; it is something to be remembered. We are invited to consider the possibility that our Purpose is our part, assigned to us by God, in God's plan. It is ours to claim (or not) from the moment we come into this physical life to the moment we complete this physical life. One distinction to consider when looking to identify our Purpose is to be aware of what fulfills and sustains us—what we are drawn to, curious about, passionate about, and have a natural talent for.

From the barista pouring the perfect latte, the doctor removing the life-threatening tumor, the chef plating the Soulful meal, to the teacher facilitating the life-changing "click" of learning, if what you are doing is nurturing our humanity in any way, you are serving in Purpose. Whether in a single moment or over a lifetime, our humanity responds to the Soul-to-Soul connections equally, expansively, and eternally.

One person holding and *sustaining* the vibration of Love can influence and raise the vibration of 750,000 people (*Power vs. Force* by David Hawkins). Even if just slightly and only for a moment, the impact is profound and the shift monumental. The Light of an authentic Soulful act has the potential to influence a healing of the darkest human moment. Can you imagine?

35) ESTABLISH AND ALIGN WITH OUR (SOUL) MISSION.

OUR SOUL MISSION: From our Soul perspective, our Mission is the format, the structure, and the vehicle on which our Soul Purpose is expressed into the world.

OUR HUMAN MISSION: From our human, physical world perspective, our Mission is a platform on which our contribution to the evolution of humanity is articulated into the world. Consider your vocation, your volunteer work, and any and all creative expression as a Mission vehicle.

Where we get distracted from remembering our Purpose is when we question what we are good at, are passionate about, and have a talent for as being unrealistic or not applicable to the "real world." Or, even more depleting, when we hold our Purpose up to what we think is noble and appropriate when comparing ourselves to the Purpose work of those who inspire us. Most people do not relate Purpose to talent, and talent to Soul, and yet, it makes total sense that talent would be an indicator of Purpose when we consider how talent is the expression of our Source through us.

For the record, everyone has a talent, a contribution, a part, and a Soul to be voiced. Remembering how our Purpose is our part, assigned to us by God in God's plan, comes in handy as a point of reference. We are all vessels for the articulation of God's creation. That is why it feels so good to be in Purpose; it's why we lose track of time and participate tirelessly for hours, finding almost superhuman-like focus, energy, and clarity. We all have Purpose and a purpose in the evolution of our humanity. The degree to which we are clear and effective in our Purpose is determined by how willing we are to allow ourselves to be informed and guided by the Source of our talent.

As an example, consider the mission statement—a staple in the development and promotion of any organization. Whether done consciously or unconsciously, when we pen a mission statement with a Soul awareness intact, we have created a declaration of intention—a claiming of Purpose. There is no "hoping" or "wanting" in the vibrational offering of an authentic mission statement. When we claim our Mission, we are fueling it with a Soul Purpose. We will be held accountable for (and be supported within the Universal Law of Attraction for) our part in our contribution.

The clarity established in a mission statement is an anchor for an organization's understanding of itself and how it intends to contribute to culture, society, and thus humanity. This articulation gives a focal point for members to rally around, check in with, and sustain their alignment with their individual and collective integrity.

It is the same with our life's Mission. Our Mission is a way for us to anchor our Purpose with a focal point of intention, a touchstone to reference sustainability of alignment and integrity. Formulate your Mission as a vehicle in which your talents are enlisted and your (Soul) Purpose is given voice into the world.

36) MANAGE OUR (SOUL) ACTIONS.

OUR SOUL ACTIONS: Managing ourselves consciously and intentionally into alignment with the remembrance of who we are as Soul—the whole, complete, and Divine extension of Source, expression of God—and bringing this awareness to our every thought, word, and action.

OUR HUMAN ACTIONS: Managing ourselves consciously and intentionally into alignment with our humanity intact for the benefit of all concerned. Consciously and intentionally aligning our thoughts, words, and actions to support our individual and, by proxy, our collective mental, emotional, physical, and spiritual health and wellness.

Allow yourself to consider the things you are drawn to, the issues you are passionate about, and the natural and developed talents you possess. Become conscious about how you feel when you are focusing on these things. What thoughts, words, and actions do you generate while you are focusing on these topics? How is your experience of yourself, and how are your feelings distinct from when you are doing something you aren't curious about or for which you have no passion or talent? How we feel about ourselves while doing what we are doing is a profound and accurate indicator of whether we are in alignment with our Purpose.

A strength of grace is present when we are doing our Purpose work. The idea that it is noble to struggle and suffer to prove ourselves worthy of being loved actually hinders our ability to be clear, unfiltered vessels of unconditional Love. By the nature of who we are as whole, complete, and Divine expressions of Source (extensions of God), we are designed to thrive and wired to evolve gloriously.

Some would suggest that by claiming we are consciously navigating our life in Soul Purpose and managing ourselves in the structure of our Soul Mission, we are abandoning common sense and are in denial of the workings of the "real world." Not so. Just because we consciously know what we know, do what we do, and Be who we Be does not exempt us from using logic and common sense to navigate our human experience. However, knowing we are managing our life with the logic and common sense of our Soul awareness makes navigating the human physical world more real, purposeful, intentional, hopeful, profound, joyful, abundant, and connected. You get the point.

When we are clear about our Purpose and grounded in our Mission, it is then up to us to manage our thoughts, words, and actions into alignment with the integrity of how we are contributing to the nurturing and evolution of our humanity. Remembering how we are doing our part assigned to us by God in God's plan, we can trust we are placed in the most appropriate position, at the most appropriate time, with the most appropriate people, and taking the most appropriate Action.

REMEMBERING AND HONORING YOUR HUMANITY as a work in progress, you are invited to implement and acclimate to these Action Points at your own pace, with patience and grace. Be firm but kind with yourself. The intention is to master your way into alignment with effective action, not to overwhelm yourself into resistance, thereby dismissing yourself to the sidelines of your potential. Love is key to mastering this process, and that includes, first and foremost, Loving yourself.

MOVING FORWARD

Whether you have stuck your toe in to test the waters of the Straight Talks, waded your way through the Talk Stories, or dove in headfirst with implementing the Action Points, you have most likely begun to understand we can no longer keep hitting the snooze button on the evolution of our humanity. It is time for us to get "real" about something: there is no such thing as the magic cure-all pill, a one-size-fits-all process that works for everyone, the one-word healing that makes us happy, the convenient answer that brings truth to our belief in (the lie of) separation, or the savior who can take care of everything for us. The work to be done in reclaiming our humanity requires we take a warrior's journey inward, owning and honing previously avoided personal accountability for everything in our lives, identifying old unconscious habits and replacing them with new habits of conscious intention, and being willing to claim and sustain our eternal At-One-Ment. No exception.

This paradigm shift in our reality, this reclaiming of our humanity that has queued us up to access our highest potential, is something we must lean into, as there is no way around it. For it is through navigating this shift consciously and intentionally that we build the mental, emotional, intellectual, physical, and spiritual strength to claim and sustain the eternal truth of who we are: whole, complete, and Divine extensions of pure positive Source energy. In this, we remember our status as Soul expressions of eternal Love, the re-membering of which informs our thoughts, words, and actions into alignment with our At-One-Ment and the reclaiming of our humanity.

This journey to reclaim our humanity, and the At-One-Ment work we are doing, is profound, and the timing is appropriate. Everything we have experienced throughout human history has led us to this time of awakening. There have been no bad choices or missed opportunities; not one wasted minute nor wrong turn. All of it, everything, has been in support of preparing us for this exponential current shift in our individual and collective consciousness. That is why it feels so intense; we are being launched forward, fueled by the energy of infinite possibility.

As is the case with any awakening process or paradigm shift, the arrival at the finish line of one destination leaves us standing at the starting line of the next level of exploration. Each time we read through the twelve chapters and check in with the thirty-six Action Points, we do so with a new perspective and a deeper appreciation for the journey, and we manifest more efficient and effective results. We are works in progress, always expanding, and in all ways evolving. There is no getting it done, and we can never get it wrong.

Avoid overanalyzing the Straight Talks and Talk Stories and over-processing the Action Points. Be assured that on a subconscious level, Who we are as a Soul knows, and remembers, our eternal At-One-Ment. With each additional review of the chapters, merely reading the words—aloud if you are willing—activates this remembrance as it works its way to a sustainable positioning at the forefront of our conscious awareness. All that is asked of us is that we continue with the fine-tuning of our At-One-Ment as a way of life to nurture the healed version of our humanity.

At-One-Ment: Reclaiming Our Humanity is not offered up as *The* answer; rather, as a foundation of (profound) insight, a launching platform for (expanded) possibility, and a life (performance) enhancing tool applicable, according to your free will, at any time and in any situation. Stick with the exploration of the Straight Talk, Talk Story, and Action Points in each of the twelve chapters, using them to inspire the exploration of your own Talk Story. Create your personal set of Action Points and further develop your Soul awareness perspective. All roads lead to Rome, and all conscious and intentional journeys lead us back to our Atonement remembered and our At-One-Ment re-membered.

Taking our place as ambassadors of humanity and doing our part with our At-One-Ment as our guide, we are making the most profound and effective contribution possible to claiming and sustaining the highest potential of our humanity fully-realized for the benefit of all concerned.

And honestly, how does it get better than that?

Go forth and be brilliant. I look forward to seeing you on the field when our paths cross, and we can visit at a café and Talk Story.

Love to you,
Peter

AT-A-GLANCE

CHAPTER REVIEW

CHAPTER ONE

It's Always Best to Start at the Beginning

-STRAIGHT TALK-

When we abandon the practice of making a conscious effort to appreciate the basics of our daily life or no longer follow the subtle signs that guide us through the world, it is absurd of us to feign confusion and disappointment. Having disconnected from our appreciation of the fundamental touchstones of daily life, we fail to recognize and claim the abundance of opportunities each moment in life has to offer. In this, we severely weaken the foundation of our humanity, and the experience of our individual and collective potential to thrive feels unattainable.

Our ability to consciously and intentionally get back to the basics of nurturing our humanity depends on our willingness to get real about how we are participating in our life—get real about what we're working with and the behaviors we accept, accommodate, and enable—starting with ourselves. Until we take 100 percent responsibility for how we are showing up in our daily life and take action to course-correct ourselves into alignment with our highest potential, we will not be in a position to contribute effectively in reclaiming our humanity—individual or collective.

−TALK STORY−

It took the events of Dorothy's journey through Oz to reassemble the aspects of her character—her mental (brain), emotional (heart), intellectual (courage), physical (human), and spiritual (Divine) bodies—into alignment with the frequency of listening that was necessary for her to hear the wisdom and profound simplicity in Glinda's guidance. Dorothy had always had the power within her to go home, to claim her mastery, to fully realize her highest potential. However, to do so in a sustainable way, she had to start from the beginning and retrain herself to be conscious and intentional with each step along her path, to be present and pay attention to the signs along the way, and to appreciate the opportunity to remember who she was as a powerful force—a tornado of creative potential. Dorothy's adventures through Oz, much like her life in Kansas, didn't happen TO her; they happened FOR her.

CHAPTER ONE ACTION POINTS
One, Two, and Three

1) PRACTICE COMMON COURTESY AND BASIC MANNERS. Implementing "Thank you" and "Please" as habitual expressions of appreciation isn't about being polite or a good person, though it sure doesn't hurt. Rather, it is all about becoming conscious of managing ourselves into a constant state of *expanded* appreciation, understanding how appreciation is one of the quickest ways to raise our "feel good" vibration. The payoff is instant and very much self-serving, as it gives us direct access to a thriving experience of ourself, our life, and thus our humanity. In this, we see how the action of reclaiming our practice of appreciation is a first step in reclaiming our humanity.

2) PAY ATTENTION TO THE BASIC SIGNS. One way to get in the practice of paying attention to the less-obvious signs the Universe is offering is to take note of the obvious signs right in front of us—literally. For example, how about becoming conscious and intentional of making complete stops at stop signs (and stoplights). The habit of making full stops at stop signs is a simple yet profound way of retraining ourselves into the practice of looking for, paying attention to, and honoring road signs, whether they be literal or figurative. This practice will assist us in developing a keener awareness of the obvious signs that have always been present, as well as becoming sensitive to the more subtle signs not so easily spotted with the human eye.

3) FINE-TUNE YOUR ATTITUDE OF GRATITUDE. Appreciation changes how we experience our world and ourselves in the world, setting us up to attract more to appreciate. Start with the things to appreciate that are right in front of you, at your fingertips—like running water. We give thanks of appreciation because, in doing so, we are connecting with and acknowledging a most abundant and generous Universe. In this, we are again holding ourselves accountable for respecting and honoring what we have. Nurturing our humanity is an inside job, starting at home and expanding outward.

CHAPTER TWO

String Training

Changing Our Mind About What Limits Us

-STRAIGHT TALK-

One definition of insanity is doing the same thing over and over and expecting different results. If we want to create something different, we have to get off our big BUTS of limited thinking and do something different.

-TALK STORY-

There is a particular technique used for training elephants that I like to use as a metaphor for how our thoughts and beliefs can keep us from realizing and achieving our full potential.

In this training, one end of a rope is tied to a hind leg of the baby elephant, and the other end is tied to a stake in the ground. The length of the rope determines the perimeter in which the baby elephant is physically able to navigate. The baby elephant, not knowing any different than what it has experienced, learns to journey no further than the tug of the rope on its leg. That world within the length of rope becomes the baby elephant's reality.

Our thoughts about what is possible, as informed by the beliefs we have inherited and own (much like the string), are only as strong as the "truth" we give them. Consider, then, that a belief is a thought that has been accepted and believed long enough to be experienced as truth. Yet if a belief is learned through repetitive thought, might it also be unlearned and replaced with a repeated new thought? And if the new thought is thought long and often enough, might it become a new belief, delivering us to a new truth, a new possibility, and a new world experience?

CHAPTER TWO ACTION POINTS

Four, Five, and Six

4) WHEN SOMETHING OR SOMEONE INSPIRES YOU, SAY SO. You never know how your acknowledgment can inform someone's awareness and inspire them to shift their perspective of Self. It's not to be nice or a good person or polite; it is so much more self-serving an art form than that. An authentic and Soul-felt acknowledgment can change the direction of an interaction instantly, course-correct it up, expand it out, and breathe life into what might otherwise be an awkward and labored experience akin to navigating birth without an epidural.

5) GET EXCITED ABOUT SOMETHING—ANYTHING. *What* you are excited about is irrelevant to *that* you are excited about something. The energy of being excited keeps us engaged, motivated, curious, and forward-focused. And it feels good, so much better than feeling disconnected, unmotivated, bored, and stagnant.

6) CLEAN YOUR NOS. This action is short and sweet. Get used to saying No like you mean it. Nothing is more confusing to people than a wishy-washy No. If you are not available or interested in saying a clear authentic Yes to something, then by all means, offer a respectful, clear, and clean "No ... thank you."

CHAPTER THREE

And the Oscar Goes To ...

-STRAIGHT TALK-

Navigating our path of At-One-Ment can be an obstacle course, awkward and clunky at first, as we trip, stumble, and fall like a toddler in the early journey of discovering balance. The key is to keep getting up and get back to it. Part of mastering the journey with grace is allowing ourselves to get it "wrong" as part of getting it "RIGHT." Each step along the way offers a lesson, an insight, and an opportunity.

-TALK STORY-

As a stage director, I invite my cast members to come to the first rehearsal bringing everything they know about life, all the tools they have developed as an actor, AND a willingness to explore the unknown. The relief the actors feel when the pressure is off to "get it right" from the first rehearsal creates a clearing for exploration and discovery. That's what rehearsals are for: to explore and play with as many options as we can imagine, harvesting golden nuggets along the way as we uncover creative genius. It's called a play for a reason.

Likewise, in the theater of life, the path to genius is laden with obstacles challenging what we already know and accept as possible, while inviting us to move through our limited thinking to explore our untapped potential. The sense of imbalance and loss of control while exploring the unknown can be confronting and uncomfortable. Initially, we feel like Bambi walking on ice for the first time, legs flailing and sliding in every direction as we awkwardly acclimate to our new environment and relationship with balance.

Remember my Oscar best-picture dinner with an 80 Proof Angel, who asked me to "promise me you will allow yourself to be awkwardly ... awesome."

CHAPTER THREE ACTION POINTS
Seven, Eight, and Nine

7) CONSIDER THAT EVERYONE WHO CROSSES YOUR PATH COULD BE AN ANGEL WITH A MESSAGE. Angels can take on many forms (not all of them have wings) and show up in the most unlikely of places (you can count on that.) So we have to be at the ready with our willingness to be present, to listen, to receive, and to appreciate. Our life experience becomes enriched when we expect the unexpected and are willing to dance with it when it shows up.

8) DEVELOP YOUR VIBE SCANNING SKILLS. Our physical eyes rarely tell us the truth about what we are looking at, and our mind is navigating our eyes through the filters of emotions informed by our past experiences. What may look to us like one thing may be something else entirely. Training ourselves to check in with our gut feeling and do what I call a vibe-check gives us a more accurate read on the situation.

9) ALLOW YOURSELF TO BE AWKWARDLY ... AWESOME. Get curious about what being awesome looks and feels like for you. You can count on this being an awkward exploration at first because you'll be navigating unfamiliar and uncomfortable territory. But what the heck, the worst that can happen is you discover something new about yourself and have Divine encounters along the way. The best that can happen is you start living your life with a "How good can I stand it?" attitude. Now that's pretty awesome.

CHAPTER FOUR
Button, Button, Who's Got the Button?

Rewiring Our Emotional Access Panel

-STRAIGHT TALK-

People may push your buttons, but remember … you installed them.

-TALK STORY-

Getting our emotional buttons pushed can be a jarring and disarming shock to the system, leaving us feeling sucker-punched and triggering any number of reactions along an expansive scale of emotions. These moments remind us of how, no matter what we know, what we do, and who we Be, we are not exempt from being accountable for managing our human emotional experience. Only when we have taken responsibility for how these buttons trigger and influence our toxic emotional reactions do we develop the ability to rewire and reprogram them to inform healthy emotional responses.

Rewiring our emotional button panel requires that we rewrite our story about each button, the people who push those buttons, and our willingness to reconsider why our buttons are available to be pushed. If we want to create something different, we have to do something different, which requires, first and foremost, that we choose to intend something different.

We cannot change the facts of our past; what has happened cannot be un-happened. So, that's the end of that. However, we can change our story about the facts, rewriting them to support a healthier, thriving version of how the data of the past informs our present and calls forth the potential of our future. I like to call this "Spinning fear into Love and living a thriving life."

CHAPTER FOUR ACTION POINTS
Ten, Eleven, and Twelve

10) SHIFT YOUR INTENTION. We see what we project onto any experience. If we want to see differently, we have to project differently. Our past-as-the-truth creates an *already-always-listening* in which we believe we know exactly how an experience will progress. Be willing to create a different experience of someone by shifting your intention about what is possible with the person. When we bring Love to any situation, we will find the Love in that situation. Be more interested in the Love than in being right. The people may still behave the way they always have; however, someone has to show up differently first to create the opportunity for change. Be willing to give up having to be right about how things always go.

11) SHIFT YOUR LISTENING. We hear what we project onto any experience. If we want to hear differently, we have to listen differently. Our past-as-the-truth creates an *already-always-listening* in which we believe we already know how an experience will play out. Be willing to have someone show up differently by shifting your intention about what is possible with the person. When we project Love onto any situation, we will find the Love in that situation. Be more interested in listening through Love than in being right. People may still say what they have always said; however, someone has to show up willing to hear something differently first to create the opportunity for a different experience. If you have to be right about something, be right about that.

12) SHIFT YOUR POTENTIAL. We create what we project onto any experience. If we want to create a different experience, we have to project the potential for a different possibility. Our past-as-the-truth creates an *already-always-listening* in which we believe we know how an experience will turn out. Be willing to create a different experience by shifting your intention about what is possible in any given situation. When we project Love onto any situation, standing in the potential to create something different, we make room for something we've never allowed ourselves to consider before. Be more interested in creating something new than in perpetuating something old.

CHAPTER FIVE

I Don't Think So!

Saying No to Energy Suckers

-STRAIGHT TALK-

Nobody takes anything from us that we do not give to them, consciously or unconsciously.

-TALK STORY-

Energy suckers are people who, doubting their potential, feed on the energy of others rather than tapping into their own life-force. Because they believe they need to feed on the energy of others, they are always on the lookout for a source of life-force to hook up to. We're not interested in being someone's energy "juice box." So, we need to be conscious and intentional about being as unattractive as possible to energy vampires. Knowing how to read people's energy and having confidence in our ability to do so is a great foundation. However, it doesn't hurt to have a little extra backup support. First, just as with the vampires in horror movies, the number one rule for energy vampires is: They have to be invited into your home to gain access. No Invite = Access Denied. Second rule: Like vampires, the energy sucker cannot see his/her reflection in a mirror. If you are not available to engage, you cannot be a source of reflection (and oh, how the energy sucker loves to gaze upon his/her reflection).

No matter how tempting it is, and the temptation is overwhelming at times, it is never appropriate for our individual or collective well-being to surrender our power over to an authority figure—whether political, religious, employer, friend, or family. A powerful teacher/leader of integrity will never ask us to surrender our personal power over to the altar of their ego. Instead, the empowering teacher/leader of integrity will stand in the fire with us—never for us—with non-attachment, holding us accountable for claiming, owning, and sustaining our highest potential fully-realized.

CHAPTER FIVE ACTION POINTS
Thirteen, Fourteen, and Fifteen

13) WHEN SOMEONE TELLS YOU WHO THEY ARE, BELIEVE THEM. As empathic beings, we are all sensitive to the energetic offering of the people we encounter. It's how we're wired. So, it would make sense to pay attention not only to the words people use and the actions they present but also to the vibrational frequency of the energy each projects. On average, most people's words, actions, and energetic offerings do not match. This contradiction can be confusing, leaving us with an unsettling feeling about someone who sounds great in words or whose actions are attractive, when the more reliable broadcast of who they are is their energetic offering. In most cases, they're not even aware they have an energetic offering, making this an even more authentic and accurate informant of their character. If the vibe is "off-putting," we can take it as a red flag of caution. Notice how I said caution, not fear. We want to be accountable for our listening (energy read) of someone—and not project our own energetic offering onto the other person, thus getting a reading of our own vibe mirrored back to us. Fear can be a projection-reflection. Caution is being conscious about the what-is of any situation.

14) TRUST YOUR VIBRATIONAL RED FLAGS. In a pocket-sized notebook, keep a record of your energy (intuitive) hits. This writing is more about creating a database of evidence to support the idea that the whole energy thing is real and to support you in building your confidence in proving to yourself how you are already skilled at being tuned-in to vibes.

15) WEAR ENERGY GARLIC. Your greatest power tool against energy suckers is your unwillingness to engage. Not out of fear, remember, but out of recognition. The last thing an energy sucker wants to do is hang out with people who've "got their number." Awareness is to the energy sucker like garlic is to the vampire. Similarly, your unwillingness to engage is to the life-force feeder like water is to the Wicked Witch of the West ... and we all know how *that* witch went down.

CHAPTER SIX

Up on Your Toes with Your Arms in the Air

"Wybieramy sie na lody!"

—STRAIGHT TALK—

With an infinite number of possibilities to choose from, what are you choosing to go with?

On some level, we've accepted the "reality" that life is hard, bad things happen to good people, and surviving through life is the best we can expect.

On some level, we also believe the truth that life is awesome, good things happen to all people, and thriving through life is our birthright.

-TALK STORY-

Recall the story of the encounter with the little boy in the Jewish Ghetto of Warsaw, Poland, who, rolling up onto his tiptoes and raising his arms in the air (appearing as if he might just leap out of his body), and with a wide-eyed angelic expression and animated unapologetic enthusiasm, announced, "Wybieramy sie na lody!" ("We're going for ice cream!").

During the years of WWII, 85 percent of the city of Warsaw was destroyed in bombing attacks. The Jewish Ghetto had been a place of fear and chaos as, daily, residents were separated and transported to any one of a number of death camps. The Warsaw of today, much of which has been rebuilt from the rubble remaining from the war, is, after thirty-plus years under Communist rule, in the early stage of reinventing itself as a democracy.

However, that day, in that moment, through the eyes of childlike wonder, Warsaw, Poland, was the happiest place on Earth because "Wybieramy sie na lody!" ("We're going for ice cream!").

CHAPTER SIX ACTION POINTS
Sixteen, Seventeen, and Eighteen

16) LEARN SOMETHING NEW ABOUT SOMEONE, SOMEPLACE, OR SOME-THING. The world is not as big as it used to be, and more and more, we are coming to see how we are all connected, whether by the internet, social media, our beliefs, or our humanity. At our human core, we all want the same things. At our Soul core, we are all at One with each other. Our Atonement, At-One-Ment, is non-negotiable, non-dismissive, all-inclusive. The more we reach out to understand each other, the more we understand how we are reaching from the same heart place for the same heart things.

17) BE WILLING TO BE INSPIRED OUT OF YOUR MIND. So much of our time, energy, and focus is given to, and exhausted by, what we think we need to get "done" in "order to" ... (fill in the blank). We can be so distracted by our past (chewing gum for the mind) and worried about our future (which, by the way, doesn't exist yet) that we aren't even present in the present, as a present. If we allow ourselves to be inspired by the "little" blessings offered up to us every day, we learn to move through our day Woke, and we won't need so many uncomfortable sledgehammer wake-up calls.

18) GO FOR ICE CREAM. Whether metaphorically or literally, go for what feeds your Spirit. Everyone loves what feeds their Spirit, whether it's music, dance, art, or ice cream (all of which are languages without borders). What feeds our individual Spirit nurtures our collective Soul.

CHAPTER SEVEN
One Thing I Know for Sure

—STRAIGHT TALK—

If I have come to know one thing for sure, it is this: We are all energetically connected as extensions and expressions of pure positive Source energy, the Source energy of everything. This energetic connection is infinite and eternal with no boundaries or disconnects. As we become more aware of and more practiced in remembering (re-membering, re-assembling) this eternal truth of who we are and our eternal connection within Source, we are better prepared and able to sustainably fuel our humanity with Love, in Love, as Love for the benefit of all concerned. Our remembrance intact, we see and experience the Oneness of ourselves, the world, and each other more accurately and authentically. We make different choices, take different actions, and create different results as we navigate our humanity from a Source awareness perspective. In our At-One-Ment, we gain unobstructed access to claiming and sustaining our humanity at its highest potential fully-realized.

−TALK STORY−

Imagine the vast ocean as Source; imagine the waves as extensions of Source. The ocean is always the ocean, and sometimes the ocean expresses itself as waves—fanning over the surface of the beach and then withdrawing back into the vast Source from which it extended. The ebb and flow of the surf is the eternal dance of the sea, just as the ebb and flow of the Soul is the eternal dance of the Source, always non-physical and sometimes expressed into physical.

We are as much connected and in this together as a humanity as we are all in this together and connected as expressions of Source, here in the physical world doing our Soul-part in support of the eternal expansion of Source. Our Souls choose a Soul Lesson curriculum to experience, and coordinate our parts and our partners with whom we will play out our Soul Agreements.

Using a theatre reference as an analogy, think of all of us as actors in a repertory theatre company of Souls. We have all been cast in various roles in a variety of productions to be performed in repertory. One night, in a musical, we could sing our way through our roles with me cast in the role of your father and you in the role of my daughter. In the next night's production, a farce, where you are cast in the role of the queen and me in the role of court jester, we enter and exit through a dozen slamming doors, catching each other in questionable states of undress. On the following night, in a comedy, we could be playing lovers, working together to navigate our mismatched families. And on the next night, in another production, a tragedy, you could be playing the role of my perpetrator, and I, playing the role of your victim, could die at your hands as the lights fade to black at the end of the first act. And so on.

In this analogy, we are all members of the same acting troupe playing various roles in various productions. We play our part in the plot of each production and give our best performance in each role. After the final curtain call, we withdraw to our dressing rooms and, while removing our costumes, wigs, and makeup, release the essence of the characters whose stories we just told. We retreat from their world, their journeys, and their thoughts, words, and actions. As actors, like Souls, we do not confuse ourselves with the roles we have played. We're storytellers; we take the journey of the play, further mastering our craft and discovering something new with each performance. When the show is over, we all go out for a post-show beer to celebrate a job well done. No longer the father/daughter, the queen/court jester, the lovers, the perpetrator/victim; we are players communing as one troupe.

Much like an actor playing a character in a live performance, the Soul, too, is playing a character in a *life* performance. Part of the actor's job is to have a big-picture understanding of their role and the evolution their character experiences as they navigate their journey of the scripted plot. However, to achieve an authentic performance, the actor must present the story as if the character he/she is portraying does not know the progression and the outcome of the plot. What the next scene holds for the character, though known by the actor, must remain unknown to that character for the play to work successfully. This knowing, too, can be said for the Soul.

CHAPTER SEVEN ACTION POINTS
Nineteen, Twenty, and Twenty-One

19) ASK THE AUTHENTIC CONSCIOUS QUESTION. Ask for clarity when you are frustrated about something and want to understand how to handle the situation or why the experience is happening. When we ask a question from the place of frustration, we get the answer that supports and matches the vibration of frustration. We get caught in a loop of one step forward, two steps back, a half-step forward, one step back, no step forward, one step back. And before long, we're only moving backward, further and further down the rabbit hole of despair. Of course, this is an unconscious process, for who in their right mind would consciously choose to remain stuck in a loop of frustration?

20) PRACTICE AN AUTHENTIC NAMASTE. Few things are more disorienting (and disturbing) than a Soulless Namaste, or as I like to call it, Faux-maste. If you're going to offer or receive a Namaste, make it a conscious, intentional, authentic Soulful experience. The Divine in me recognizes and honors the Divine in you. Integrity is key.

21) BE THE CHANGE YOU WISH TO SEE IN THE WORLD. We cannot control other people or external events. We can, however, control how we are showing up in our thoughts, words, and actions. In fact, how we choose to show up is the *only* thing we can control. When we remember who we are as whole, complete, and Divine, we show up in the world as an asset rather than a liability, an inspiration for the change we desire.

CHAPTER EIGHT
The Retrograde Phenomenon

Walking Through the Chaos with the Strength of Grace

-STRAIGHT TALK-

Shift happens. There is no way around it; the only way is through it. What determines the state of our well-being when we come out the other side is influenced and informed by who we choose to Be while walking through the shift storm.

-TALK STORY-

Natural phenomena take place. It's the natural order of things. We can work with them, or we can work against them. We're going to experience these phenomena, there's no way around them, and we do not control them—hard as we may try. The only way for us is *through* the experience. The better prepared we are, the more effectively and efficiently we navigate the process. In this, earthquakes and retrogrades are also similar. We can't control them; however, we can choose to what degree we are controlled by them.

CHAPTER EIGHT ACTION POINTS
Twenty-Two, Twenty-Three, and Twenty-Four

22) DROP, COVER, AND HOLD. Basic earthquake survival training includes an understanding and implementation of the Drop, Cover, and Hold technique: (1) Drop to the floor, (2) get under Cover of a solid surface or up against a weight-bearing wall, and (3) Hold your hands over your head and stay where you are. During a retrograde, a similar practice can be implemented: (1) Drop the need to control, (2) Cover yourself in a bubble wrap of Love, and (3) put a Hold on making any major decisions.

In the midst of a retrograde experience is not the time to create anything new. This is the time to take stock of what we have and where we are and to count our blessings. This process will distract us from relating to the drama of the moment as the truth of what is possible beyond the moment.

23) SHOW UP, SUIT UP, AND SHUT UP. During retrograde or anytime we feel unbalanced, uneasy, and vulnerable, it is important for us to get focused, get clear, and listen. This is not the time to attempt to make sense of the chaos—that will only expand the experience of chaos. This is not the time to be scattered in thoughts, words, and actions that will only create frustration from unfulfillable intentions.

Our focus, like a disco ball reflecting light in all directions, would be better served to be more like a laser beam: focused in one direction and aimed at one subject. As silly as it may sound, retrograde is a great time to work on that coloring book for grown-ups that we purchased on an intuitive hunch.

During chaotic and stressful times, we may feel like pulling out our "invisibility cloaks" and getting off the grid. Yet if we check out, we miss the opportunity to consciously and intentionally be present to what this experience is showing us, the seeing of which will change everything. Suiting up isn't about checking out of the experience but rather about checking into what the experience is providing. To do this, we need to avoid getting caught up in the chaos-as-truth and be willing to ride out the storm with the intention to arrive intact to the clear skies on the other side. This is where suiting up in our protective gear and wrapping ourselves in things that make us feel safe, cozy, and protected—wearing natural fabrics, listening to soothing music, eating organic foods, drinking an abundance of filtered water, etc.—will serve us well in feeling connected and protected.

24) DO WHAT EVERY GOOD GIRL SCOUT AND BOY SCOUT WOULD DO.

Be prepared. Have a Retrograde Survival Kit well-thought-out and appropriately stocked. If we know that meditation and prayer help us stay connected and grounded, set the intention to do either, or both, more frequently and consistently during the retrograde. If we know that watching funny movies keeps our spirits light, we can have a list of movies at the ready. If we believe in the power of chocolate, we can stock up on a box of sixty assorted Godiva truffles with a ratio favoring dark chocolate raspberry (just sayin'). The point is: do what works for you.

Like any other cycle experience, if we know what we need to support us for the duration of the experience, we can have these supplies at the ready. When we make it a priority to be familiar with what we need to feel grounded and supported during a retrograde, we find ourselves going into the experience with a sense of focus, clarity, and grounding. This preparedness can make all the difference in how we not only navigate the duration of the retrograde but also how we benefit from the experience once we have reached the clearing on the other side. We will feel less unbalanced, less uneasy, and less vulnerable. And, there will be far fewer mental, emotional, and physical messes to clean up.

CHAPTER NINE
Couture Esprit

Dress Your Spirit

-STRAIGHT TALK-

Dressing to express your Spirit is a way of announcing to the world that you know who you are. It doesn't cost a million dollars to look like a million bucks. You could walk into a room wearing a gunny sack and, with your spirit-light on high, could be the best-dressed person at the ball. On the other hand, even the highest-end couture can't compensate for a depleted Spirit. If the contents don't match the wrapping ... well, it's like I always say, "You can sprinkle powdered sugar over a pile of poo and call it dessert, but it's still a pile of poo."

-TALK STORY-

Diversity is what makes life an interesting, rich, and full-spectrum experience. If we all look alike, think alike, and act alike, the fashion industry would die, online retailers would crumble, and finding our car in the parking lot of the Mall of America would be a total nightmare. Like black-and-white photography, we need contrast to ignite imagination, fuel expression, and jump-start curiosity.

I am reminded of the story about the white canvas on display in an art exhibit and the artist explaining his vision to a curious observer. When asked by the observer, "What am I looking at?" the artist explains, "A cow eating grass." "Where is the grass?" the observer inquires. "The cow ate it all," the artist proclaims. "Where is the cow?" the observer protests. "Off looking for more grass," the artist insists.

The experience of art is relative. The purpose of art is not to dictate an experience but rather to inspire an experience, to provide the opportunity for an experience to be had. In getting a reaction, in triggering a response, the blank canvas and the canvas exploding with color and light both do their job.

Like the canvas on which the artist is inspired to express himself or herself, people are canvases on which the Soul is inspired to express its Self. Just as an infinite number of Souls express themselves into the world, there are an infinite number of "people canvases" onto and through which these expressions are projected. I like to think of the world as an art gallery and everyone on the planet an original work of art, a unique Soul expression.

"Vivé la France."

CHAPTER NINE ACTION POINTS

Twenty-Five, Twenty-Six, and Twenty-Seven

25) DON'T JUDGE A BOOK BY ITS COVER. IT JUST MIGHT BE THE BEST BOOK YOU'LL EVER READ. (This is an expanded version of earlier action points intended to support changing our perspective.) Consider that, though our eyes reveal to us what we are seeing, it is our heart that informs what we see. If we are looking at the world through the mind filters of our past, we are only seeing a fraction of what we are looking at. We are only seeing the parts of what we are looking upon that match what our mind filters will allow us to identify as real, facts, and truth. If we allow ourselves to see with our Spirit eyes, with our heart, we will get a more accurate read on the subject while, at the same time, expanding our vision beyond the borders of our filters. How often have we judged something as "what is," only to find how mistaken we were when we changed our mood, emotion, or perspective. In other words, when we changed our mind. There was a time when the masses not only thought but *believed* the Earth was flat. We know now that is not the case. Not because the Earth changed its shape but because we've changed our perspective (which changed what we thought were the facts, which changed our truth about the Earth). When our beliefs about the Earth changed from flat to round, our whole world opened up beyond anything we previously imagined possible.

26) BE WILLING NOT TO FIT IN. This practice can be tricky if we need to be validated by others. Throughout history, many seers have been criticized, ridiculed, and martyred because they spoke openly about what they were able to see that the masses could not. When we see through Spirit eyes and trust what our heart shows us, fitting in can be an intense experience. When we have the confidence to trust what we see, we release any need to fit in, and we no longer seek validation from others. Not to suggest that we give the masses the "bird" but rather to be so self-sufficient that we don't care, give power to, or limit our potential because of what anybody thinks. This isn't about isolating ourselves from the rest of the world. Rather, this is about establishing a balance between navigating the world of the "spiritually-vision-impaired" and the "clear-seeing through Spirit eyes." It's not one or the other; it's a mastery of both. The ego may fear the experience of standing alone in the crowd, yet when we look at the world through Spirit eyes, we feel more connected to everyone and everything than we ever did when we were trying to fit in.

27) DRESS YOUR SPIRIT. Fashion is all about making a statement. Whether we do it consciously or unconsciously, how we dress is an announcement to the world about how we think (or don't think) about ourselves. Now, this isn't about dressing yourself to prove to the world who you are pretending to be, or trying to convince people who you are, or proving a point. We've all had the experience of seeing someone enter a room "dressed to the nines" and looking like a million bucks on the outside, but something about their vibe just didn't match. You couldn't put your finger on it, but something was wrong. Remember, you can sprinkle powdered sugar on a pile of poo and call it dessert, but it still stinks. And then there are people who walk into a crowded room, their authentic Spirit intact, inner light shining brightly—they could be wearing a burlap sack and still look like a million bucks.

Looking like a million bucks doesn't have to cost a million bucks. This is about accessorizing your Spirit, not maxing your credit card. Whether you're wearing a simple piece of jewelry, a colorful silk scarf, a funky pair of thrift-store shoes, a whimsical hand-painted necktie, or an imported sporty wristwatch, never leave the house without first checking in the mirror to see that you are wearing your Spirit right-side-out. The key is to dress authentic to *your* Spirit. Love is in the details.

CHAPTER TEN

What About My NO Aren't You Getting?

And, How May I Help You with That?

-STRAIGHT TALK-

Until we master our use of the powerful No! we cannot and will not call forth its counterpart, the authentic Yes! Working together, they are power tools for creating and sustaining the integrity of our individual and collective humanity through more effective and efficient communication. The unbalanced energy of a disempowered No and an inauthentic Yes generates chaos and confuses everyone. The clean and straightforward vibration of the powerful No and the authentic Yes are key to establishing the foundation of internal confidence from which we engage the trust and clear-listening of the people we are enrolling as co-creators of our atonement and the reclaiming of our humanity.

-TALK STORY-

WHAT MAKES A NO POWERFUL?

A powerful No comes from a place of clarity grounded in an abiding respect and Love of ourself and, by proxy, everyone. Established in a set of personal boundaries and an unshakeable commitment to our individual and collective health and wellness, the powerful No is confident, unapologetic, and clean. When we take a stand in the energy of our powerful No, no one is confused, especially and foremost ourself. The powerful No responds rather than reacts.

WHAT CONSTITUTES AN AUTHENTIC YES?

An authentic Yes, like the powerful No, comes from a place of clarity grounded in an established set of personal boundaries, an unshakeable commitment to our individual and collective health and wellness, and an abiding respect and Love of ourself and, by proxy, everyone. The authentic Yes is confident, unapologetic, and clean. When we take a stand in the energy of our authentic Yes, no one is confused, especially and foremost ourself.

CHAPTER TEN ACTION POINTS

Twenty-Eight, Twenty-Nine, and Thirty

28) WHEN YOU SAY NO, MEAN IT. By itself, your No has no power. Like all words, it is a symbol. It is the energy and clarity behind the No that breathes life into it and gives it power. If your No is uncertain, hesitant, apologetic, manipulative, controlling, resistant, or not-worthy, not only will you confuse others, but you, yourself, will be confused by the less-than-desirable results you are manifesting.

29) WHEN YOU HEAR NO, GET IT. When we accept and honor someone's No, the person feels heard and respected. The key is to honor the person's No, complete the interaction, and move on.

30) PRACTICE THE CONSCIOUS AND INTENTIONAL YES. When your Yes is grounded in "for-the-benefit-of-all-concerned" and fueled with the life-force of Love, the entire Universe is queued up to support you with everything you need to navigate a fully-realized experience and manifest expansive results— beyond what you know to be possible.

CHAPTER ELEVEN

When We Change Our Mind, We Can Change Our World

-STRAIGHT TALK-

With advancements in technology, science, and medicine, we are sitting on a gold mine of human potential unlike anything we have ever seen before. With the sacred institutions of religion and government, we can create and establish the foundation on which to launch and sustain the next expression of our evolved human potential. With this profound potential comes profound responsibility; with this sacred structure comes sacred accountability. The measure of both is determined by the integrity of our humanity.

-TALK STORY-

The state of our humanity informs our experience of the world rather than our world informing our humanity. With our humanity intact, we create thriving advances in our human experience, the likes of which we could only have previously imagined. Without our humanity intact, we generate a self-imposed survival of our human experience, the likes of which we would not have dared to imagine. We use the same tools to create both experiences. However, the tools themselves only construct the symbols of our potential. It is the state of mind and intention behind the use of these tools that inform thriving or surviving results.

To make the shift from unconscious naivety to conscious intention, it is imperative that we consider what we are working with—the tools we are using to create our reality and manifest our highest potential. As is the case with any tool, it is important to understand its purpose and potential, how to use it safely and effectively, and to be clear on what we intend to achieve. Much like a chef's knife, picked up by the handle, it is an artisan's tool; picked up by the blade, it becomes a self-inflicting assault weapon. Social media, science, and medicine are profound tools with expansive potential. Like any tool, they can be a power tool for thriving or an assault weapon of self-destruction, depending on how we use them, the power we give them, and the intention with which we use them. Our reclaimed and nurtured humanity is the foundation on which we launch the effectiveness of any tool we use to evolve and expand our experience. The choice is ours.

With a change of mind, we can use the internet to nurture and advance our humanity while holding ourselves accountable for managing our use for the benefit of all concerned as our number one priority, responsibility, and desire. With a redefining of purpose, we can reap the profound benefits of science as it continues to support us in understanding the workings of the Universe and our place in the bigger picture. With a shift in consciousness and reclaiming our mind-over-matter potential, we can redirect our medical research to address diseases at their source and develop preventative medicinal options. With a reconnection to our faith as an expression of our Source, we breathe the life of Divine back into our religion. When We the People act for the benefit of all concerned, electing vetted representatives who are a vibrational match for our self-nurtured humanity, we can navigate effective politics and efficient governing through the full spectrum of our evolutionary process. The key to all of this is held in how we manage our individual and, by proxy, our collective humanity. Shift internally, act locally, manifest globally.

CHAPTER ELEVEN ACTION POINTS
Thirty-One, Thirty-Two, Thirty-Three

31) BE AN ONLINE ADVOCATE FOR HUMANITY AT ITS BEST. Social media can be a power tool for humanity **or** an assault weapon for its downfall. We only need a basic understanding of the Law of Attraction to make this connection. It's not rocket science or brain surgery: What we focus on, we attract. To this point, it is our free will to create whatever we choose, and we do, whether consciously or unconsciously. The Universe does not distinguish between good or bad, right or wrong, high or low.

The Universe is a Yes machine. Whatever we give our focus to, it says Yes to.

32) UPDATE YOUR INTERNAL WIRING BY DOING MORE OF WHAT YOU LOVE. Begin taking steps to become a cooperative component in your mental, emotional, physical, and spiritual wellness. The best preventative medicine is to do more of what you Love. Most diseases are diagnosed well into the manifestation of the disorder, suggesting that most diseases are unconsciously manifested and become a conscious experience only after being diagnosed. This perspective makes sense, for who in their right mind would consciously create a disease? Doing more of what we Love as a way of life is a more preventative than reactive form of medicine.

33) PRAY AND VOTE IN ALIGNMENT WITH YOUR HIGHEST GOOD. When we pray in fear, we can only attract and hear answers and guidance that match our fear. This is so, not because our prayers are unworthy of being heard and answered by a punitive and exclusivist God—good heavens no. Our prayers are always answered by an all-Loving and all-Powerful Creator. We just can't hear the all-Loving and all-Powerful voice of the Creator when we are locked into fear-listening.

The same can be said for how we cast our vote. We vote for the candidate and issues that are the closest vibrational match for our chronic vibrational mindset. We vote to elect messengers to represent us in the political and governing structure. The personalities we elect to office could then be likened to mirrors of our collective mindset: poster children for the chronic cultural mindset.

Bottom line: Be conscious and intentional to check in with your emotional and vibrational offering *before* launching your prayer and casting your vote. Aim high for the benefit of all concerned. Understand that like attracts like, and we can raise the vibration of our offering with the confidence that we are cooperative components in manifesting the highest potential of our humanity.

CHAPTER TWELVE
At-One-Ment

The Soul of Our Humanity

-STRAIGHT TALK-

Our journey through *At-One-Ment: Reclaiming Our Humanity* has reconnected us with the importance, value, and influence of the role our conscious (and unconscious) participation plays in our evolution as a human race. We have reawakened to the awareness of how our experience is always a direct reflection, reaction, and response to how we are showing up and navigating our thoughts, words, and actions. We have been reminded of the gift of our free will and the influence our chronic vibrational offering has in creating what we focus on, whether we want it or not. Understanding how we show up, participate, and promote the nurturing of our human potential is our power tool, putting at our fingertips access to our humanity's infinite possibility.

-TALK STORY-

Key to the success of our efforts is understanding how our humanity is an inside job. We do not change the world by manipulating, controlling, and forcing external influences. This way of Being only distracts us from being effective and diminishes our efforts, leaving us fatigued, depleted, and defeated. We have never created anything we wanted from an unvetted, fear-driven, survival perspective. We have always created what we want when we do so from a conscious and intentional commitment for the benefit of all concerned, always and in all ways, no exceptions.

HUMANITY

1: compassionate, sympathetic, or generous behavior
or disposition: the quality or state of being humane

2: the quality or state of being human

Our humanity is always (and in all ways) present within our individual and collective potential. However, the degree to which it is nurtured, practiced, and mastered is our free will. When we get distracted by the self-imposed workings of the "real" world (and let's be straight about this: they *are* self-imposed), our humanity can get displaced to the back burner of our awareness. Its eternal pilot light ignited and always at a simmer, our humanity is never unavailable for liberation and expression. The key to the mastery of our humanity at its highest potential is to move it to the forefront of our awareness as a conscious and intentional articulation of who we believe ourselves to Be.

SOUL

1: the immaterial essence, animating principle,
or actuating cause of an individual life

2: the spiritual principle embodied in human beings,
all rational and spiritual beings, of the universe

3: a person's total self

4: the moral and emotional nature of human beings

5: spiritual or moral force

We are invited here to consider the possibility that our humanity is a vehicle on which our Soul expresses itself. When our humanity is in alignment with this awareness, we have a healthy, Soulful experience of ourselves and our world. When our humanity is out of alignment with this awareness, we have a dis-eased, Soulless experience of ourselves and our world. In this, we might say that the state of our humanity is an expression of Soul consciousness.

For the sake of this conversation and the intention of establishing a common ground on which to rally, let us consider how we are all whole, complete, and Divine extensions of Source, expressions of God. The life-force that is Source, God, is the same life-force that animates our human physical bodies. It is the life-force that is projected into our physical body at the beginning of our physical life and retracted from our physical body upon the completion of our physical life experience. This life-force is pure positive Source energy, eternal and Divine by design, always non-physical, and sometimes expressed in the physical.

When we allow ourselves to consider, even for a moment, our Source/God connection, we see and experience ourselves in the Light of our Truth. From this perspective, we are positioned to see and experience everyone and everything in the Light of this Truth. When we allow ourselves to sustain our perspective in this awareness, we generate thoughts, words, and actions in alignment with our Source connection. In other words, we see and experience ourselves, everyone, and everything Soul to Soul in the frequency of Love.

ATONEMENT

1: the exemplifying of human(ity's) oneness with God

This concept can be confronting for the human intellect and ego to wrap around, to the point of inducing resistance in the form of mild to extreme retaliation. Throughout human history, humans have fought against humans to prove separation is the truth, all the while ignorant to the Truth that separation is impossible. The pain inflicted and experienced in the name of being "right" is induced without considering how, being expressions of the same Source, whatever we do to another, we do to ourselves, and whatever we do to ourselves, we do to the collective. There is no mystery here. It's pretty straightforward when we know what we're working with and do so with an open heart and a clear, intentional mind.

Considering how what we do to ourselves, we do to the collective, we can see how our humanity is an inside job—establishing a conscious relationship with our internal emotional, mental, physical, and spiritual alignment. Our understanding of Self as "Soul having a human experience" and bringing this awareness to our thoughts, words, and actions positions us to be most effective and efficient in our contribution to the evolution of humanity.

AT-ONE-MENT

We as One

To be clear, it is important to understand there is no way on earth, literally, that everyone will be on the same page, frequency, perspective, agenda, or intention for any sustainable amount of time. That is not only unrealistic, but it is also not appropriate given the purpose of the human experience—and its contribution to the evolution of the Soul while navigating Soul Lessons and Soul Agreements. Humanity and the world at large are a work in progress. As stated in previous chapters, this isn't about reaching a goal and riding it out for all eternity. Diversity, contrast, and change are our strengths: they are what make this life and this world interesting. Can you imagine a world filled with stagnant, like-minded people walking around with perpetual blissed-out expressions on their faces? Honestly, how long would that be interesting before we needed to stir things up to feel alive?

Contrast, which fuels creativity, is key to the richness of the human experience. Given that we are creative beings—expressions of our Creator and participating in a creative work in progress—contrast is our creative power tool. When we navigate our human creative process with our Soul aware-ness perspective intact, we create humanity at its magnificent potential. When we attempt to navigate this same process in the absence of our Soul awareness, creativity becomes an assault weapon manifesting struggle, hardship, despair, and inhu-manity. Both paths are valid given our Source birthright of free will. However, we need only dwell in the shadow side of the creative process long enough to identify what we do *not* desire so that we can be inspired to identify what we *do* desire, pivot our focus, and course-correct our efforts in the direction of the Soulful potential of each experience. There is no need to take up residence in the shadow side of any experience beyond its purpose of inspiring us otherwise. Unless, of course, we choose to overstay its Divine purpose. We have a choice.

However, whatever we choose, we need to get real about having exercised our free will to choose and get clear about our part in this process, our individual contribution, and hold ourselves accountable for having chosen to participate in alignment (or out of alignment) with the Soul of our humanity at its best.

CHAPTER TWELVE ACTION POINTS
Thirty-Four, Thirty-Five, Thirty-Six

34) RE-MEMBER OUR PURPOSE BY REMEMBERING WHO WE ARE.

REMEMBER OUR SOUL PURPOSE: From our Soul perspective, our Purpose is to remember who we are as the whole, complete, and Divine expression of Source, an extension of God. That's it, that's all there is to it, and that is the ALL of it.

REMEMBER OUR HUMAN PURPOSE: From our human, physical world perspective, our Purpose is the projection of our Soul Purpose in the form of our contribution to the evolution of humanity: what we bring to the world to nurture, inspire, and evolve.

35) ESTABLISH AND ALIGN WITH OUR (SOUL) MISSION.

OUR SOUL MISSION: From our Soul perspective, our Mission is the format, the structure, and the vehicle on which our Soul Purpose is expressed into the world.

OUR HUMAN MISSION: From our human, physical world perspective, our Mission is a platform on which our contribution to the evolution of humanity is articulated into the world. Consider your vocation, your volunteer work, and any and all creative expression as a Mission vehicle.

36) MANAGE OUR (SOUL) ACTIONS.

OUR SOUL ACTIONS: Managing ourselves consciously and intentionally into alignment with the remembrance of who we are as Soul—the whole, complete, and Divine extension of Source, expression of God—and bringing this awareness to our every thought, word, and action.

OUR HUMAN ACTIONS: Managing ourselves consciously and intentionally into alignment with our humanity intact for the benefit of all concerned. Consciously and intentionally aligning our thoughts, words, and actions to support our individual and, by proxy, our collective mental, emotional, physical, and spiritual health and wellness.

REMEMBERING AND HONORING YOUR HUMANITY as a work in progress, you are invited to implement and acclimate to these Action Points at your own pace, with patience and grace. Be firm but kind with yourself. The intention is to master your way into alignment with effective action, not to overwhelm yourself into resistance, thereby dismissing yourself to the sidelines of your potential. Love is key to mastering this process, and that includes, first and foremost, Loving yourself.

AT-ONE-MENT: RECLAIMING OUR HUMANITY

AT-A-GLANCE

Action Point Checklist

PART ONE: BACK TO BASICS
Action Points

1. Practice common courtesy and basic manners.
2. Pay attention to the basic signs.
3. Fine-tune your Attitude of Gratitude.
4. When something or someone inspires you, say so.
5. Get excited about something—anything.
6. Clean your Nos.
7. Consider that everyone who crosses your path could be an angel with a message.
8. Develop your vibe scanning skills.
9. Allow yourself to be awkwardly … awesome.

PART TWO: SHIFTING THE PARADIGM

Action Points

10. Shift your intention.

11. Shift your listening.

12. Shift your potential.

13. When someone tells you who they are, believe them.

14. Trust your vibrational red flags.

15. Wear energy garlic.

16. Learn something new about someone, someplace, or something.

17. Be willing to be inspired out of your mind.

18. Go for ice cream.

PART THREE: CLAIMING OUR POTENTIAL
Action Points

19. Ask the authentic conscious question.
20. Practice an authentic Namaste.
21. Be the change you wish to see in the world.
22. Drop, Cover, and Hold.
23. Show up, suit up, and shut up.
24. Do what every good Girl Scout and Boy Scout would do.
25. Don't judge a book by its cover. It just might be the best book you'll ever read.
26. Be willing *not* to fit in.
27. Dress your Spirit.

PART FOUR: MASTERING OUR HUMANITY

Action Points

28. When you say No, mean it.

29. When you hear No, get it.

30. Practice the conscious and intentional Yes.

31. Be an online advocate for humanity at its best.

32. Update your internal wiring by doing more of what you Love.

33. Pray and vote in alignment with your highest good.

34. Re-member our Purpose by remembering who we are.

35. Establish and align with our (Soul) Mission.

36. Manage our (Soul) Actions.

ACKNOWLEDGMENTS

Curtain Call of Appreciation

MUCH LIKE THE CURTAIN CALL AT the end of a performance, this assembly of acknowledgments is a celebration of the players who have contributed profoundly to the creative journey of bringing *At-One-Ment: Reclaiming Our Humanity* to the world stage. The generous words of support, encouragement, and guidance offered by each person provided the foundation on which I was able to build, nurture, and launch this passion project, this vehicle on which my purpose work is given voice and expressed into the world. For this village of believing eyes, I am eternally grateful.

To my clients who have participated in classes, workshops, and private sessions over the years—your contributions continue to lift up our work together to new and glorious heights. And, to the friends and colleagues who bring the gift of insight and example to our every visit—you inspire me to reach for the stars and embrace the heavens.

To Mare App, Millete Birhanemaskel, and the team at Whittier Cafe; to Kathleen Davis, Noreen Doyle, Susan and Larry Gordon, Marc Graham and Laura Main, Kenny Herring, Del, Linda and Alex Hunter, John Lake, Robyn Momper, Christian Munck, Ann Oberbroeckling, David Racine, Lee Goodfriend, and the staff at Racine's; and to Bob Ragland, Kathy Thompson, and Gregg Schroeder—your contributions to this process, consciously or unconsciously, have been profound in ways you may never fully understand. Thank you.

To my mentors Billie Daniel and Frank Zwolinski, who saw a spark of potential earlier on and provided a platform to find and express my voice, nurture and develop my talents, and tap into my inner-leader—thank you for keeping the torch of my potential lit until I was ready and able to claim it for myself.

To my mind, body, and spirit health and wellness facilitators: Steve Axtell, Monica Bottagaro, Cuky Choquette Harvey, Rachel Louden, Mia Scott, and Marnie Vincolisi—thank you for holding me accountable for keeping my feet on the ground, my head on straight, and my heart wide open.

To the team of readers and editors fondly referred to as the Book Doulas: Diane Ahonen, John Ashton, Sue Bigus, Sonia Choquette, Shane Delavan, Helen Hand, Dianne Maroney, Sydney Price, and Marianne Wunch—your diverse perspectives and variety of masteries kept this journey on course during our climb to the mountaintop. For this, I am profoundly grateful.

To the team at My Word Publishing: Jennifer Jas, Rich Wolf, and Victoria Wolf—thank you for taking my hand and guiding me through the publishing process. The respect and integrity with which you embraced the words, concepts, and message provided the perfect space to iron out the wrinkles and fine-tune the finishing touches before sending this baby into the world.

To my in-laws for welcoming this quirky-theatre-spiritual guy into your tribe—you may not have always wrapped your minds around the details of my journey, yet I have always felt wrapped in the warmth of your love and laughter. Thank you for that.

To my parents, siblings, nieces, and nephews for the honor of taking this Earth journey together—our Soul Agreement contracts read much like an enthusiast's sushi order, an all-you-can-eat array of life lessons. Thank you for the opportunity to find my way to who I am and what I'm made of.

To my master teachers Sonia Choquette and (Mama) Sonia P Choquette—hungry to see what you saw and know what you know, when you said "Jump," I trusted you enough to ask, "How high?" Thank you for holding me accountable for claiming my place and taking my seat at the Master's table.

To my dear Lady Jane Stanfield, your believing eyes, love, and support meant the world to me during our time together on Earth. And now, I can feel your continued support and guidance from Heaven. You are the belle of the ethereal ball always and in all ways.

To my husband, best friend, and the love of my life Shane Delavan—when we said "I do," I don't think either of us had any idea the path the Universe had mapped out for us. There is no one else I would rather be on this journey with making our way through each moment soul to soul, heart to heart, hand in hand.

Head Shot – Eric Weber Photographer
at ericweberstudios.com

Back Cover Photo – Meghan Ralph,
Solar Radiant Photography

Cover Design – Victoria Wolf at
wolfdesignandmarketing.com

ABOUT THE AUTHOR

PETER J HUGHES is a master life-change facilitator with on-the-court experience leading workshops and classes and coaching private clients since 2004. Peter draws on his thirty years of professional theatre experience as a stage director and production manager, along with his training as a professional intuitive and spiritual teacher, to "pull to the forefront of your life your most fully-realized performance." People who have worked with Peter, both on stage and off, and no matter their beliefs or their relationship to spirituality, are touched by the light and love he emanates. Peter's delightful and often wicked sense of humor, direct yet loving guidance, and old-soul wisdom help make waking up to our higher potential a nurturing as well as powerful transition.

"Our work together is informational, inspirational, and transformational, leading you to the doorway of your highest potential fully-realized." — Peter J Hughes

For more information, please visit www.peterjhughes.com.

Made in the USA
Las Vegas, NV
12 October 2021